RabbitMQ Essentials
Second Edition

Build distributed and scalable applications with message queuing using RabbitMQ

Lovisa Johansson
David Dossot

BIRMINGHAM - MUMBAI

RabbitMQ Essentials
Second Edition

Copyright © 2020 Packt Publishing

Commissioning Editor: Kunal Chaudhari
Acquisition Editor: Aditi Gour
Content Development Editor: Nathanya Dias
Senior Editor: Ayaan Hoda
Technical Editor: Utkarsha S. Kadam
Copy Editor: Safis Editing
Project Coordinator: Aishwarya Mohan
Proofreader: Safis Editing
Indexer: Tejal Daruwale Soni
Production Designer: Alishon Mendonca

First published: April 2014
Second edition: August 2020

Production reference: 1070820

Published by Packt Publishing Ltd.
Livery Place
35 Livery Street
Birmingham
B3 2PB, UK.

ISBN 978-1-78913-166-6

www.packt.com

Packt.com

Subscribe to our online digital library for full access to over 7,000 books and videos, as well as industry leading tools to help you plan your personal development and advance your career. For more information, please visit our website.

Why subscribe?

- Spend less time learning and more time coding with practical eBooks and Videos from over 4,000 industry professionals

- Improve your learning with Skill Plans built especially for you

- Get a free eBook or video every month

- Fully searchable for easy access to vital information

- Copy and paste, print, and bookmark content

Did you know that Packt offers eBook versions of every book published, with PDF and ePub files available? You can upgrade to the eBook version at www.packt.com and as a print book customer, you are entitled to a discount on the eBook copy. Get in touch with us at customercare@packtpub.com for more details.

At www.packt.com, you can also read a collection of free technical articles, sign up for a range of free newsletters, and receive exclusive discounts and offers on Packt books and eBooks.

About the authors

Lovisa Johansson has been working daily with RabbitMQ for many years. Through CloudAMQP, the company 84codes offers managed RabbitMQ clusters. With 50,000+ running instances, they are considered to be the largest provider of RabbitMQ as a Service in the world. Lovisa is an experienced developer with a Master's degree in Computer Science and Engineering. Through her work, she continues to write the most popular and widespread educational content about RabbitMQ, and occasionally shares this knowledge as a speaker at various conferences.

The insights of this book are thanks to the advanced skills and experience of the team at 84codes, founded in Sweden in 2012. The 84codes team is highly experienced in the benefits, challenges, and opportunities of message queue architecture. We dedicate ourselves to providing developers with a simple cloud infrastructure, which has made this book possible. Special thanks to the experts who contributed valuable knowledge, including Anton Dalgren, Daniel Marklund, Elin Vinka, Andrew Evans and Angela Olson.

David Dossot has worked as a software engineer and architect for more than 18 years. He has been using RabbitMQ since 2009 in a variety of different contexts. He is the main contributor to the AMQP transport for Mule. His focus is on building distributed and scalable server-side applications for the JVM and the Erlang VM. He is a member of IEEE, the Computer Society, and AOPA, and holds a diploma in Production Systems Engineering from ESSTIN.

He is a Mule champion and a DZone Most Valuable Blogger. He commits on multiple open source projects and likes to help people on Stack Overflow. He's also a judge for the annual Jolt Awards software competition.

About the reviewer

Héctor Veiga Ortiz is a software engineer specializing in real-time data applications. Recently, he has focused his work on different cloud technologies like AWS and Kubernetes, to develop and run scalable, resilient, and high-performing systems that are able to handle high-volume, real-time data. He has a Master's degree in Telecommunication Engineering from the Universidad Politécnica de Madrid, and a Master's degree in Information Technology and Management from the Illinois Institute of Technology. He currently works at HERE Technologies, where he develops scalable applications to serve real-time traffic data worldwide. Héctor is also the technical reviewer of *RabbitMQ Cookbook*, and has authored *Akka Cookbook*, both for Packt Publishing.

Packt is searching for authors like you

If you're interested in becoming an author for Packt, please visit `authors.packtpub.com` and apply today. We have worked with thousands of developers and tech professionals, just like you, to help them share their insight with the global tech community. You can make a general application, apply for a specific hot topic that we are recruiting an author for, or submit your own idea.

Table of Contents

Preface

RabbitMQ is a message broker, providing a communication structure between components and services. Thanks to the **Advanced Message Queuing Protocol** (**AMQP**) and all available RabbitMQ client libraries, most major programming languages and services are able to work together seamlessly, in an asynchronous manner.

This book explores the powerful possibilities of RabbitMQ by delving into the basic fundamentals through the user journey of **Complete Car** (**CC**), a fictitious taxi dispatch company with real-life user requirements.

Who this book is for

If you are a professional enterprise developer or someone who just codes for fun, *RabbitMQ Essentials* is a valuable resource on open source message queue architecture. Even those who are already familiar with microservices and messaging will discover value in reading this book for an exploration of moving forward with best practices and resource efficiency. This book will give you the push you need to get started with creating new and exciting applications or migrating existing monoliths to a microservice architecture.

What this book covers

Chapter 1, *A Rabbit Springs to Life*, is an introduction to RabbitMQ, how to get started, and the benefits of message queues. The chapter then instructs you on how to install and configure RabbitMQ and the preparation for going forward with developing applications.

Chapter 2, *Creating a Taxi Application*, discusses the creation of a simple taxi order application using RabbitMQ. By the end of this chapter, expect to have an understanding of how to connect to RabbitMQ, publishing with direct and topic exchanges, and consuming messages from queues. The chapter also explains message acknowledgments and negative acknowledgments (acks and nacks).

Chapter 3, *Sending Messages to Multiple Taxi Drivers*, moves on with the CC project, providing information on the prefetch value settings, which control the number of messages that are being sent to the consumer at the same time. This chapter also covers how consumers can manually acknowledge messages, recommendations for developing a zero-message loss design, and how to receive messages without acknowledgments. The chapter closes by providing you with a good understanding of the fanout exchange.

Chapter 4, *Tweaking Message Delivery*, is about message **time-to-live** (**TTL**), using message property name expiration, and other important topics about tweaking message delivery, including dead-letter exchanges and queues.

Chapter 5, *Message Routing*, dives deeper into message flow, covering how to respond to a sender and how header exchange can be used to perform the property-based routing of messages. Additionally, request-response styles of interactions are also explained.

Chapter 6, *Taking RabbitMQ to Production*, presents different strategies that can be used to deal with the failure of a RabbitMQ broker. Topics include clustering, quorum queues, and federation. This chapter also covers a very important aspect of RabbitMQ – log processing and data analysis.

Chapter 7, *Best Practices and Broker Monitoring*, funnels down all the great information in the preceding chapters into best practices and key takeaways that can be used in real-world application development. This final chapter also explains common errors in RabbitMQ and provides strategies to put in place to monitor system performance and avoid catastrophic situations.

To get the most out of this book

How to install RabbitMQ on Ubuntu and via Docker is explained in Chapter 1, *A Rabbit Springs to Life*. It also gives suggestions about how to set up a hosted version of RabbitMQ through CloudAMQP.

The code in the book is easy to follow even if you are not familiar with Ruby or Python. All the code examples in Ruby have been tested using Ruby 2.7, and all the code examples in Python have been tested using Python 2.7, on macOS. However, they should probably work with future version releases too.

Software/hardware	OS requirements
Python 2.7 Ruby 2.7 A web browser	macOS Ubuntu

If you are using the digital version of this book, we advise you to type the code yourself or access the code via the GitHub repository (link available in the next section). Doing so will help you avoid any potential errors related to the copying and pasting of code.

Download the example code files

You can download the example code files for this book from your account at
www.packt.com. If you purchased this book elsewhere, you can visit
www.packtpub.com/support and register to have the files emailed directly to you.

You can download the code files by following these steps:

1. Log in or register at www.packt.com.
2. Select the **Support** tab.
3. Click on **Code Downloads**.
4. Enter the name of the book in the **Search** box and follow the onscreen instructions.

Once the file is downloaded, please make sure that you unzip or extract the folder using the latest version of:

- WinRAR/7-Zip for Windows
- Zipeg/iZip/UnRarX for Mac
- 7-Zip/PeaZip for Linux

The code bundle for the book is also hosted on GitHub at https://github.com/
PacktPublishing/RabbitMQ-Essentials-Second-Edition. In case there's an update to the code, it will be updated on the existing GitHub repository.

We also have other code bundles from our rich catalog of books and videos available at https://github.com/PacktPublishing/. Check them out!

Download the color images

We also provide a PDF file that has color images of the screenshots/diagrams used in this book. You can download it here: https://static.packt-cdn.com/downloads/
9781789131666_ColorImages.pdf.

Conventions used

There are a number of text conventions used throughout this book.

`CodeInText`: Indicates code words in text, database table names, folder names, filenames, file extensions, pathnames, dummy URLs, user input, and Twitter handles. Here is an example: "As it stands, neither the `cc-admin` nor `cc-dev` users have permission to do anything on `cc-dev-vhost`."

A block of code is set as follows:

```
connection = Bunny.new ENV['RABBITMQ_URI']
# Start a session with RabbitMQ
connection.start
```

Any command-line input or output is written as follows:

```
sudo apt install curl gnupg -y
sudo apt install apt-transport-https
```

Bold: Indicates a new term, an important word, or words that you see onscreen. For example, words in menus or dialog boxes appear in the text like this. Here is an example: "Click on the **Admin** tab of the console."

Warnings or important notes appear like this.

Tips and tricks appear like this.

Get in touch

Feedback from our readers is always welcome.

General feedback: If you have questions about any aspect of this book, mention the book title in the subject of your message and email us at customercare@packtpub.com.

Errata: Although we have taken every care to ensure the accuracy of our content, mistakes do happen. If you have found a mistake in this book, we would be grateful if you would report this to us. Please visit www.packtpub.com/support/errata, selecting your book, clicking on the Errata Submission Form link, and entering the details.

Piracy: If you come across any illegal copies of our works in any form on the Internet, we would be grateful if you would provide us with the location address or website name. Please contact us at copyright@packt.com with a link to the material.

If you are interested in becoming an author: If there is a topic that you have expertise in and you are interested in either writing or contributing to a book, please visit authors.packtpub.com.

Reviews

Please leave a review. Once you have read and used this book, why not leave a review on the site that you purchased it from? Potential readers can then see and use your unbiased opinion to make purchase decisions, we at Packt can understand what you think about our products, and our authors can see your feedback on their book. Thank you!

For more information about Packt, please visit packt.com.

A Rabbit Springs to Life 1

Messaging or **message queuing** is a method of communication between applications or components. Thanks to message queues, these applications can remain completely separate as they process their individual tasks. Messages are typically small requests, replies, status updates, or even just information. A message queue provides a temporary place for these messages to stay, allowing applications to send and receive them as necessary.

RabbitMQ is an open source message broker that acts as the intermediary or middleman for independent applications, giving them a common platform to communicate. RabbitMQ mainly uses an Erlang-based implementation of the **Advanced Message Queuing Protocol** (**AMQP**), which supports advanced features such as clustering and the complex routing of messages.

This chapter includes information about how to get started with RabbitMQ, and why it would benefit an architecture. This book follows a fictitious taxi agency, **Complete Car** (**CC**), to demonstrate how they have implemented RabbitMQ into the architecture. This chapter shows how to install and configure RabbitMQ so that it's easy to get everything up and running.

This chapter will cover the following topics:

- Explaining message queues
- Discovering AMQP and RabbitMQ
- Using RabbitMQ in real life
- Exploring the benefits of message queuing
- A RabbitMQ scenario
- Getting ready for RabbitMQ

Let's get started!

Technical requirements

The code files of this chapter can be found on GitHub at h
ttps://github.com/PacktPublishing/RabbitMQ-Essentials-Second-
Edition/tree/master/Chapter01.

Explaining message queues

Smoke signals, couriers, carrier pigeons, and semaphores: if this was a riddle, the word
messages would immediately spring to mind. Humanity has always had the need to
connect, finding new ways to defy challenges posed by the distance between the different
groups of people needing to communicate. Humankind has come a long way with modern
technologies, but essentially, the basics remain. Senders, recipients, and messages are at the
core of all our communication infrastructures.

Software applications have the same needs; systems need to communicate and send
messages between each other. They sometimes need to be sure that the message that's been
sent has reached its destination, and sometimes they need to receive an immediate
response. In some cases, they may even need to receive more than one response. Based on
these different needs, different styles of communication between systems have emerged.

AMQP, RabbitMQ's default protocol, is explained in the next section.

Discovering AMQP and RabbitMQ

Message queuing is a one-way communication style that provides asynchronous interaction
between systems. As this chapter continues to describe how message queues work, the
benefits will become clear. Some background on the request-response message exchange
pattern will shed light on how RabbitMQ works.

The request-response message exchange pattern

There are many types of message exchange patterns, but the request-response style is the
most common. A system, acting as a client, interacts with another remote system, which is
acting as a server. The client sends a request for data, and the server responds to the
request, as shown in the following diagram:

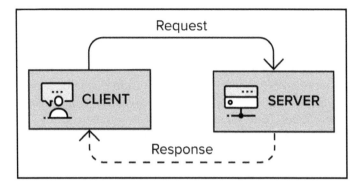

Fig 1.1: The request-response interaction between the client and the server

The request-response style is used when the client must have an immediate response or wants the service to complete a task without delay, such as being placed on hold when calling a restaurant to reserve a table:

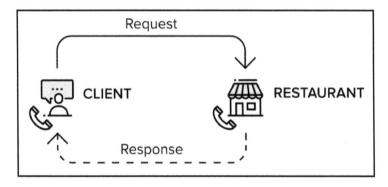

Fig 1.2: Request-response between a client and a restaurant

Whether it takes the form of a remote procedure call, a web service invocation, or consumption of a resource, the model is the same: one system sends a message to another and waits for the remote party to respond. Systems communicate with each other in a point-to-point manner, where events and processes occur simultaneously or have dependencies or events related to time; the interaction between the client and server is **synchronous**.

One on hand, this request-response style gives developers a simple programming model as everything happens procedurally. On the other hand, the tight coupling between both parties has a deep impact on the architecture of the whole system as it is hard to evolve, hard to scale, and hard to ship in independent releases.

Message queuing exchange pattern

Message queuing is a one-way style of interaction where one system asynchronously interacts with another system via messages, generally through a message broker. A requesting system in asynchronous communication mode does not wait for an answer or require return information; it continues processing no matter what. The most common example of such an interaction is an email. The point is, asynchronous communication does not involve waiting for a response in order to continue processing. In fact, there may be no response or it may take some time for a response to be sent. Whatever the case, the system does not rely on a response to continue the process.

Messages flow in one direction, from the publisher to the broker and finally to the consumer:

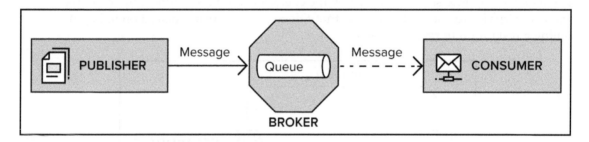

Fig 1.3: Basic components of a one-way interaction with message queuing

Systems and applications play both the role of message publishers (producers) and message consumers (subscribers). A publisher publishes a message to a broker that they rely on to deliver the data to the intended consumer. If a response is required, it will arrive at some point in time through the same mechanism, but reversed (the consumer and producer roles will be swapped).

A loosely coupled architecture

One big advantage of the messaging queuing approach is that systems become loosely coupled with each other. They do not need to know the location of other nodes on the network; a mere name is enough to reach them. Systems can, therefore, be evolved in an independent manner with no impact on each other as the reliability of message delivery is entrusted to a broker.

The following diagram illustrates a loose coupling between the publisher and the consumer:

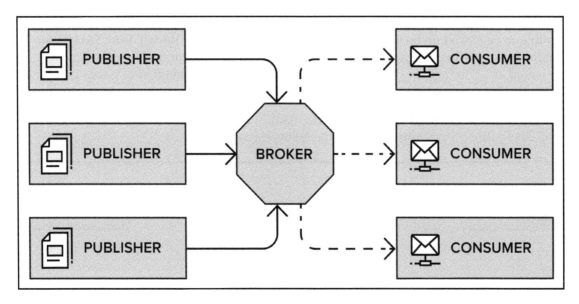

Fig 1.4: Message queuing enabling a loosely coupled architecture

If one system is down for any reason, the other part of the system can still operate, and messages that are supposed to be sent between them wait in the queue.

The architecture represented via message queuing allows for the following:

- The publishers or consumers can be updated one by one, without them impacting each other.
- The performance of each side leaves the other side unaffected.
- The publishers or consumers are allowed to fail without impacting each other.
- The number of instances of publishers and consumers to scale and to accommodate their workload in complete independence.
- Technology mixing between consumer and publishers.

The main downside of this approach is that programmers cannot rely on the mental model of procedural programming where events occur one after another. In messaging, things happen over time. Systems must be programmed to deal with this.

If all this is a little blurry, use the example of a well-known protocol, **Simple Mail Transfer Protocol** (**SMTP**). In this protocol, emails are published (sent) to an SMTP server. This initial server then stores and forwards the email to the next SMTP server, and so on until the recipient email server is reached. At this point, the message is queued in an inbox, waiting to be picked up by the consumer (typically, via POP3 or IMAP). With SMTP, the publisher has no idea when the email will be delivered or whether it will eventually be delivered at all. In the case of a delivery failure, the publisher is notified of issues later down the line.

The only sure fact is that the broker has successfully accepted the message that was initially sent. This entire process can be seen in the following diagram:

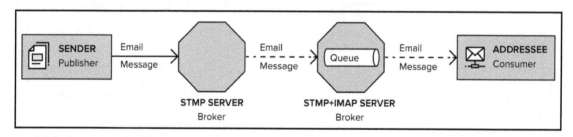

Fig 1.5: The email infrastructure as an analogy for message queuing

Furthermore, if a response is needed, it will arrive asynchronously using the same delivery mechanism but with the publisher and consumer roles reversed.

With these fundamental notions established, it is the perfect time to delve into the messaging protocol that will be used in this book, which is AMQP.

Meet AMQP

AMQP is an open standard protocol that defines how a system can exchange messages. The protocol defines a set of rules that needs to be followed by the systems that are going to communicate with each other. In addition to defining the interaction that happens between a consumer/producer and a broker, it also defines the representation of the messages and commands being exchanged. AMQP is truly interoperable as it specifies the wire format for messages, leaving nothing open to interpretation by a particular vendor or hosting platform. Since it is open source, the AMQP community is prolific and has broker and client implementations in a wide range of languages.

RabbitMQ is built upon the AMQP 0-9-1 specification, but plugins are available that support AMQP 1.0.

 The AMQP 0-9-1 specification can be downloaded at `http://www.rabbitmq.com/resources/specs/amqp0-9-1.pdf`.

The following is a list of the core concepts of AMQP, which will be explained in detail in upcoming chapters:

- **Broker or message broker**: A broker is a piece of software that receives messages from one application or service, and delivers them to another application, service, or broker.
- **Virtual host, vhost**: A vhost exists within the broker. It's a way to separate applications that are using the same RabbitMQ instance, similar to a logical container inside a broker; for example, separating working environments into development on one vhost and staging on another, keeping them within the same broker instead of setting up multiple brokers. Users, exchanges, queues, and so on are isolated on one specific vhost. A user connected to a particular vhost cannot access any resources (queue, exchange, and so on) from another vhost. Users can have different access privileges to different vhosts.
- **Connection**: Physical network (TCP) connection between the application (publisher/consumer) and a broker. When the client disconnects or a system failure occurs, the connection is closed.
- **Channel**: A channel is a **virtual connection** inside a **connection**. It reuses a connection, forgoing the need to reauthorize and open a new TCP stream. When messages are published or consumed, it is done over a channel. Many channels can be established within a single connection.
- **Exchange**: The exchange entity is in charge of applying routing rules for messages, making sure that messages are reaching their final destination. In other words, the exchange ensures that the received message ends up in the correct queues. Which queue the message ends up in depends on the rules defined by the exchange type. A queue needs to be bound to at least one exchange to be able to receive messages. Routing rules include direct (point-to-point), topic (publish-subscribe), fanout (multicast), and header exchanges.
- **Queue**: A queue is a sequence of items; in this case, messages. The queue exists within the broker.
- **Binding**: A binding is a virtual link between an exchange and a queue within the broker. It enables messages to flow from an exchange to a queue.

The following diagram illustrates an overview of some of the concepts in AMQP:

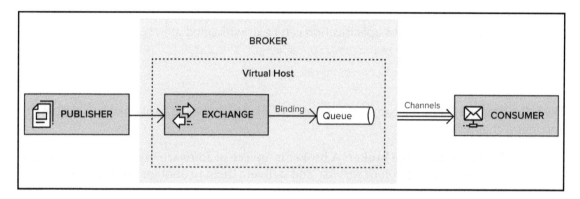

Fig 1.6: Overview of some of the concepts defined by the AMQP specification

The open source broker shown in detailin this book has been built from the ground up to support AMQP, but many other protocols are also supported by RabbitMQ, such as MQTT, HTTP, and STOMP.

Now, it's time to turn the focus to RabbitMQ.

The RabbitMQ broker

RabbitMQ is an Erlang implementation of an AMQP broker. It implements Version 0-9-1 of AMQP with custom extensions, as allowed by the protocol. Erlang has been chosen because of its intrinsic support for building highly reliable and distributed applications. Indeed, Erlang is used to run telecommunication switches in several large telecommunication systems, and a total system's availability of nine nines has been reported (that's only 32 milliseconds of downtime per year). Erlang is able to run on any operating system.

For data persistence, RabbitMQ relies on Mnesia, the in-memory/file-persisted embedded database of Erlang. Mnesia stores information about users, exchanges, queues, bindings, and so on. The queue index stores message positions and information on whether a message has been delivered or not. Messages are stored either in the queue index or in the message store, a key-value store shared among all queues.

For clustering, it mainly relies on Erlang's ingrained clustering abilities. RabbitMQ can easily be extended with the addition of plugins. For example, a web-based administration console can be deployed on RabbitMQ thanks to this mechanism.

Plugins can be used to extend the core broker functionality. There are many plugins available for RabbitMQ, and it's also possible to develop plugins, if needed: `https://www.rabbitmq.com/plugins.html`.

RabbitMQ can be set up on a single, standalone instance, or as a cluster on multiple servers:

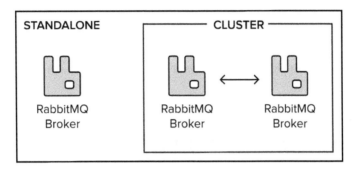

Fig 1.7: Standalone instance, or as a cluster on multiple servers

RabbitMQ brokers can be connected together using different techniques, such as federation and shovels, in order to form messaging topologies with smart message routing across brokers and the capacity to span multiple data centers.

The following screenshot shows federation between RabbitMQ brokers located in different places around the world:

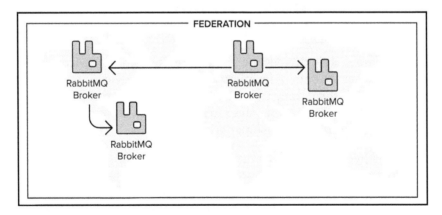

Fig 1.8: The RabbitMQ broker engaging in various topologies

RabbitMQ supports AMQP 1.0 through plugins.

 AMQP 1.0 was published at the end of 2011 after the development and maintenance of AMQP was transferred to OASIS. AMQP has been drastically revised between 0-9-1 and 1.0. This was so drastic that some core concepts, such as the exchange, no longer exist. Thus, AMQP 1.0 is a different protocol than 0-9-1, but there is no truly compelling reason to adopt it. It is not more capable than 0-9-1, and some would also argue that it has lost some of the key aspects that made it attractive in the first place.

So, when or where is RabbitMQ used? The next section describes some common use cases for RabbitMQ.

Using RabbitMQ in real life

The most common use case for RabbitMQ is a single producer, single consumer queue. Think of it as a pipe where one application puts messages into one end of the pipe and another application reads the messages that come out the other end. Messages are delivered in first in, first out order. These messages may be commands or contain important data. This sounds easy, but where could this type of architecture be applied? It's time to understand when and why message queuing shines!

Message queues between microservices

Message queues are often used in between microservices, but what does that mean?

Microservice architectural style divides the application into small services, with the finished application being the sum of its microservices. The services are not strictly connected to each other. Instead, they use, for example, message queues to keep in touch. One service asynchronously pushes messages to a queue and those messages are delivered to the correct destination when the consumer is ready.

The microservice architecture is often compared and contrasted with the monolith architecture, where the entire system is bundled together into one piece of software. One application is not only responsible for a particular task; it actually performs every step needed to complete a particular function. Monoliths communicate within the system since all the parts are running in the same process. This system is highly coupled since every function is reliant on the others.

In an example of a webshop built on a monolith architecture style, one system handles all of the functions, including inventory, payments, reviews, and ratings and so on, as shown in the following diagram:

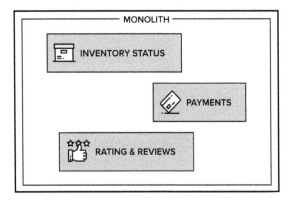

Fig 1.9: A webshop built in a monolith architecture style

A webshop built on the microservice architecture, on the other hand, means that each part of the system is an individual activity. One microservice handles reviews and ratings. Then, there's another inventory, and then yet another for payments, and so on, as shown in the following diagram:

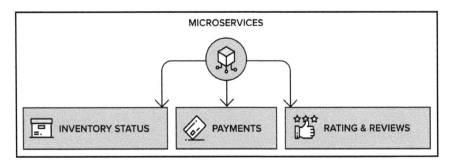

Fig 1.10: A microservice architecture style where each part is focused on a single business capability

Each pair of requests and responses communicates independently. This is known as stateless communication. While many microservices are involved, they are not directly dependent on each other.

Another typical use case for RabbitMQ is as a task queue, which we'll cover in the next section.

Event and tasks

Events are notifications that tell applications when something has happened. One application can subscribe to events from another application and respond by creating and handling tasks for themselves. A typical use case is when RabbitMQ acts as a task queue that handles **slow** operations.

Let's take a look at two examples of this:

- Imagine a social media application such as Instagram. Every time someone publishes a new post, the network (followers) needs to be informed about the new post. This could be a very time-consuming operation. Millions of people could be trying to perform the same task at the same time. The application can, with the use of message queues, enqueue a task onto the queue for each post as it arrives. When the worker receives the request, it retrieves a list of followers for the sender, and updates each of them.

- As another example, think of an email newsletter campaign tool that is sending out thousands of emails to thousands of users. With a possible scenario where many users trigger bulk messages at the same time. The email newsletter campaign tool needs to be able to handle this volume of messages. All these emails can be added to a push queue with instructions to the worker regarding what to send and to whom. Every single email is handled, one by one, until all the emails have been sent.

The following diagram shows a task queue, where messages are first entering the queue, and then handled. New tasks are then added to another queue:

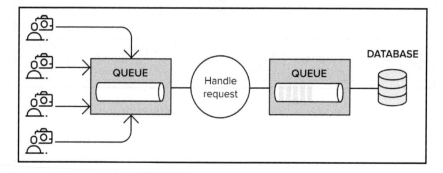

Fig 1.11: Event and task queue

With that, we've looked at and reviewed two typical use cases. The benefits of RabbitMQ have been apparent in each. We'll make this even more evident by exploring the benefits of message queuing in the next section.

Exploring the benefits of message queuing

Communication between various applications plays an important role in distributed systems. There are many examples of when a message queue can be used, so let's highlight some features and benefits of message queuing in microservice architectures:

- **Development and maintenance made easier**: Dividing an application across multiple services allows separate responsibilities and gives developers the freedom to write code for a specific service in any chosen language. It will be easier to maintain written code and make changes to the system; when updating a single authentication scheme, only the authentication module must have code added for testing, without it disrupting any other functions.
- **Fault isolation**: A fault can be isolated to a single module and will thereby not affect other services. For example, an application with a reporting service temporarily out of function will not affect the authenticate or payment services. As another example, making changes to the reporting service still allows customers to perform essential transactions, even when they aren't able to view reports.
- **Enhanced levels of speed and productivity**: Different developers are able to work on different modules at the same time. In addition to speeding up the development cycle, the testing phase is also impacted by the use of microservices and message queues. This is because each service can be tested on its own to determine the readiness of the overall system.
- **Improved scalability**: Microservices also allow for effortless scale-out at will. It's possible to add more consumers if the message queue is growing. Adding new components to just one service is easy to do without changing any other service.
- **Easy to understand**: Since each module in a microservice architecture represents a single functionality, getting to know the relevant details for a task is easy. For example, hiring a consultant for a single service does not require them to understand the entire system.

Now that is enough knowledge to be dangerous, so it is a good time to dive into the RabbitMQ scenario company that sets the scene for the rest of this book.

A RabbitMQ scenario

CC is a new taxi agency with huge potential. Today, the company has just two taxi drivers and two developers, but they want to expand a lot in the upcoming year. CC has already built a website in Ruby and started out with a backend, also written in Ruby, that stores CC trips in a database. CC also has some scripts, written in Python, that generate route reports.

So far, CC's system runs as follows:

- The company's website and blog runs on Ruby.
- The Rich Internet Application that stores route data, such as the starting point and the endpoint of the trip, is written in Ruby.
- There's a back-office that sends route updates to drivers and is written in Ruby.
- Multiple ad hoc Python scripts are used to extract and message data to generate route reports.
- Taxi applications are written in Python.

The old architecture is illustrated as follows:

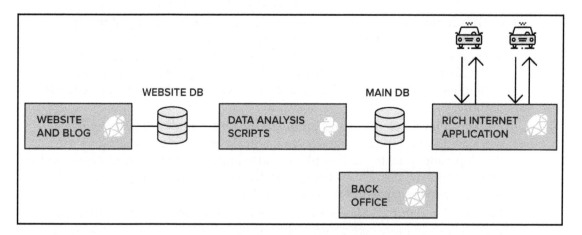

Fig 1.12: CC software landscape

Why is CC looking at adding RabbitMQ to an already busy environment? The main reason is because of a new feature CC wants to offer to their customers – they want to build a taxi application that handles reservations on the go. CC also wants to be able to scale painlessly. The plan is to build an app where users can book a car via a smartphone, receive booking confirmation, and view the car approaching the starting point of the trip.

Since CC already has some services in different languages, and since CC wants to be able to scale easily, they decided to use a ready-made message-oriented middleware such as RabbitMQ for asynchronous communication between the app, the client, and the backend.

As CC's knowledge and usage of RabbitMQ increases, they will discover new opportunities to leverage it in the environment. For now, let's follow CC as it gets started with its very first step into working with RabbitMQ.

Getting ready for RabbitMQ

To get started, the following three installation and configuration steps need to be completed:

- Installing the RabbitMQ broker
- Installing the management plugin (Web UI)
- Configuring the vhost and user

Let's start by installing the broker!

Installing the broker

CC runs its production servers on Ubuntu Linux. One developer has macOS and Linux, while the other one is all Windows. This heterogeneity is not a concern for RabbitMQ, which can run natively on all these operating systems.

RabbitMQ provides complete online installation guides for all the supported operating systems, and they can be found here: `http://www.rabbitmq.com/download.html`. This book contains instructions for Debian/Ubuntu, where RabbitMQ is installed from the `apt` repository. It also contains instructions for Docker further down in this chapter.

RabbitMQ installation on Ubuntu

There are relatively few steps required to install RabbitMQ. They are as follows:

1. Update Ubuntu.
2. Download and install the repository key.
3. Ensure the key is in the repository.
4. Install RabbitMQ from the package repository.

Ensure that Ubuntu is up to date before starting the download process. Make sure that the operating system is using the latest versions of all software since outdated dependencies create security vulnerabilities.

Run the `apt update` command to download the latest releases of the installed software:

```
apt upgrade
```

RabbitMQ requires several software packages. Verify that `curl`, `apt-transport-https`, and `GnuPG` are on the system by running the following command:

```
sudo apt install curl gnupg -y
sudo apt install apt-transport-https
```

The `-y` option accepts any licenses for these dependencies. Ubuntu installs all required sub-packages.

Discover the name of the operating system by running any of the following commands:

- `cat /etc/os-release`
- `lsb_release -a`
- `hostnamectl`

The release name is non-technical. Previous names include `focal` and `bionic`. Ubuntu does not include RabbitMQ by default, so it must be added to the repository key before you proceed. Execute the following set of commands in a Terminal:

```
curl -fsSL
https://github.com/rabbitmq/signing-keys/releases/download/2.0/rabbitmq-rel
ease-signing-key.asc
sudo apt-key add -
sudo tee /etc/apt/sources.list.d/bintray.rabbitmq.list <<EOF
deb https://dl.bintray.com/rabbitmq-erlang/debian [os release name] erlang
deb https://dl.bintray.com/rabbitmq/debian [os release name] main
EOF
```

These commands download the key and add it to the repository list before adding the appropriate operating system packages for the broker and Erlang.

RabbitMQ is written in Erlang, a functional language that has robust built-in support for creating distributed networks. The developers maintain a list of minimum versions (`https://www.rabbitmq.com/which-erlang.html`) of the language for the latest supported releases of the broker. At the time of writing, RabbitMQ 3.8 supports Erlang 21.3 through 23.

RabbitMQ can now be installed correctly.

Though not absolutely required for using RabbitMQ, it is encouraged to discover this powerful language and platform. You can learn more about Erlang at `http://www.erlang.org/`. Alternatively, you can consider Elixir as an optional language for the Erlang **virtual machine** (**VM**). You can find out more about this at `http://elixir-lang.org`.

Run the following commands to install RabbitMQ:

```
sudo apt install -y rabbitmq-server
sudo apt install librabbitmq-dev
```

The `librabbitmq-dev` library includes a client for interacting with the broker. However, the server may be the only requirement.

RabbitMQ installation on Docker

Docker containers allow the separation and control of resources without risking corrupting the operating system. Instructions for installing Docker are available from the official website: `https://docs.docker.com/get-docker/`. With Docker installed, pull the RabbitMQ image:

```
docker pull rabbitmq
```

Run the broker with reasonable defaults:

```
docker run -d --hostname my-rabbit --name my-rabbit -p 5672:5672 -p
15672:15672 -e RABBITMQ_ERLANG_COOKIE='cookie_for_clustering' -e
RABBITMQ_DEFAULT_USER=user -e RABBITMQ_DEFAULT_PASS=password  --name some-
rabbit rabbitmq:3-management
```

A Docker container needs to be created so that it's accessible from the `localhost` with the management console enabled. This will be discovered shortly.

Starting RabbitMQ

Installing the RabbitMQ server from the repository also installs a suite of command-line tools used to start the server for the first time. This is done by executing the following command:

```
rabbitmq-server start
```

The server starts in the foreground. To run the broker as a service, use the following commands:

```
sudo systemctl enable rabbitmq-server
sudo systemctl start rabbitmq-server
sudo systemctl status rabbitmq-server
```

The `systemctl` command can also be used to manage services in Ubuntu. The output of the final command should show that the broker is running. Consult the RabbitMQ documentation (`https://www.rabbitmq.com/troubleshooting.html`) if not.

Downloading the example code

Download all the example code files for this book. They can be purchased from `http://www.packtpub.com`. If you purchased this book elsewhere, visit `http://www.packtpub.com/support` and register to have the files emailed to you directly.

Verifying that the RabbitMQ broker is running

Now, verify that the RabbitMQ broker is actually working by using the `status service` command.

Write the following line in the Terminal:

```
$ sudo service rabbitmq-server status
  rabbitmq-server.service - RabbitMQ broker
   Loaded: loaded (/lib/systemd/system/rabbitmq-server.service; enabled;
vendor preset: enabled)
  Drop-In: /etc/systemd/system/rabbitmq-server.service.d
           └─10-limits.conf, 90-env.conf
   Active: active (running) since Mon 2019-04-29 13:28:43 UTC; 1h 43min ago
  Process: 27474 ExecStop=/usr/lib/rabbitmq/bin/rabbitmqctl shutdown
(code=exited, status=0/SUCCESS)
 Main PID: 27583 (beam.smp)
   Status: "Initialized"
    Tasks: 87 (limit: 1121)
   CGroup: /system.slice/rabbitmq-server.service
           ├─27583 /usr/lib/erlang/erts-10.2.2/bin/beam.smp -W w -A 64 -
MBas ageffcbf -MHas ageffcbf -MBlmbcs 512 -MHlmbcs 512 -MMmcs 30 -P 1048576
-t 5000000
           ├─27698 /usr/lib/erlang/erts-10.2.2/bin/epmd -daemon
           ├─27854 erl_child_setup 1000000
           ├─27882 inet_gethost 4
           └─27883 inet_gethost 4

Apr 29 13:28:42 test-young-mouse-01 rabbitmq-server[27583]:  ##  ##
Apr 29 13:28:42 test-young-mouse-01 rabbitmq-server[27583]:  ##  ##
RabbitMQ 3.7.14. Copyright (C) 2007-2019 Pivotal Software, Inc.
Apr 29 13:28:42 test-young-mouse-01 rabbitmq-server[27583]:  ##########
Licensed under the MPL.  See https://www.rabbitmq.com/
Apr 29 13:28:42 test-young-mouse-01 rabbitmq-server[27583]:  ######  ##
```

```
Apr 29 13:28:42 test-young-mouse-01 rabbitmq-server[27583]:    ##########
Logs: /var/log/rabbitmq/rabbit@test-young-mouse-01.log
Apr 29 13:28:42 test-young-mouse-01 rabbitmq-server[27583]:
/var/log/rabbitmq/rabbit@test-young-mouse-01_upgrade.log
Apr 29 13:28:42 test-young-mouse-01 rabbitmq-server[27583]:
Starting broker...
Apr 29 13:28:43 test-young-mouse-01 rabbitmq-server[27583]: systemd unit
for activation check: "rabbitmq-server.service"
Apr 29 13:28:43 test-young-mouse-01 systemd[1]: Started RabbitMQ broker.
Apr 29 13:28:43 test-young-mouse-01 rabbitmq-server[27583]:   completed with
9 plugins.
```

> The default folders where the package has installed files are
> /etc/rabbitmq for configuration files, /usr/lib/rabbitmq for
> application files, and /var/lib/rabbitmq for data files (mnesia).

Look at the running processes for RabbitMQ and find both the service wrapper and the
Erlang VM (also known as BEAM) that's running, as follows:

$ pgrep -fl rabbitmq
```
27583 beam.smp
```

$ ps aux | grep rabbitmq
```
ubuntu   10260  0.0  0.1  14856  1004 pts/0     S+   15:13   0:00 grep --
color=auto rabbitmq
rabbitmq 27583  0.5  8.5 2186988 83484 ?        Ssl  13:28   0:36
/usr/lib/erlang/erts-10.2.2/bin/beam.smp -W w -A 64 -MBas ageffcbf -MHas
ageffcbf -MBlmbcs 512 -MHlmbcs 512 -MMmcs 30 -P 1048576 -t 5000000 -stbt db
-zdbbl 128000 -K true -- -root /usr/lib/erlang -progname erl -- -home
/var/lib/rabbitmq -- -pa /usr/librabbitmq/lib/rabbitmq_server-3.7.14/ebin
-noshell -noinput -s rabbit boot -sname rabbit@test-young-mouse-01 -boot
start_sasl -config /etc/rabbitmq/rabbitmq -kernel
inet_default_connect_options [{nodelay,true}] -sasl errlog_type error -sasl
sasl_error_logger false -rabbit lager_log_root "/var/log/rabbitmq" -rabbit
lager_default_file "/var/log/rabbitmq/rabbit@test-young-mouse-01.log" -
rabbit lager_upgrade_file "/var/log/rabbitmq/rabbit@test-young-
mouse-01_upgrade.log" -rabbit enabled_plugins_file
"/etc/rabbitmq/enabled_plugins" -rabbit plugins_dir
"/usr/lib/rabbitmq/plugins:/usr/lib/rabbitmq/lib/rabbitmq_server-3.7.14/plu
gins" -rabbit plugins_expand_dir "/var/lib/rabbitmq/mnesia/rabbit@test-
young-mouse-01-plugins-expand" -os_mon start_cpu_sup false -os_mon
start_disksup false -os_mon start_memsup false -mnesia dir
"/var/lib/rabbitmq/mnesia/rabbit@test-young-mouse-01" -kernel
inet_dist_listen_min 25672 -kernel inet_dist_listen_max 25672
rabbitmq 27698  0.0  0.1   8532  1528 ?         S    13:28   0:00
/usr/lib/erlang/erts-10.2.2/bin/epmd -daemon
rabbitmq 27854  0.0  0.1   4520  1576 ?         Ss   13:28   0:00
```

```
erl_child_setup 1000000
rabbitmq 27882  0.0  0.1   8264  1076  ?        Ss   13:28   0:00
inet_gethost 4
rabbitmq 27883  0.0  0.1  14616  1808  ?        S    13:28   0:00
inet_gethost 4
```

It is possible that, when RabbitMQ runs, a process named epmd is also running. This is the Erlang port mapper daemon, which is in charge of coordinating Erlang nodes in a cluster. It is expected to start even if the clustered RabbitMQ application is not running.

Note that by default, the broker service is configured to auto-start when the Linux host starts.

Skip the hassle of the installation and configuration of RabbitMQ and use a hosted RabbitMQ solution. CloudAMQP is the largest provider of hosted RabbitMQ clusters: www.cloudamqp.com.

Installing the management plugin (Web UI)

RabbitMQ does not install a management console by default, but the optional web-based plugin used in this example makes it easy to peek into a running RabbitMQ instance.

The Debian package installs several scripts. One of them is rabbitmq-plugins. Its purpose is to allow us to install and remove plugins. Use it to install the management plugin, as follows:

```
$ sudo rabbitmq-plugins enable rabbitmq_management
Enabling plugins on node rabbit@host:
rabbitmq_management
The following plugins have been configured:
  rabbitmq_consistent_hash_exchange
  rabbitmq_event_exchange
  rabbitmq_federation
  rabbitmq_management
  rabbitmq_management_agent
  rabbitmq_shovel
  rabbitmq_web_dispatch
Applying plugin configuration to rabbit@host...
The following plugins have been enabled:
  rabbitmq_management
  rabbitmq_management_agent
  rabbitmq_web_dispatch
```

Yes, it is that easy!

Use a web browser to reach the home page of the management console by navigating to `http://<hostname>:15672`, as shown in the following screenshot:

Fig 1.13: The login screen of the management console

Stay tuned for the next episode – creating and configuring users!

Configuring users

One of the scripts that's installed by the Debian package is `rabbitmqctl`, which is a tool for managing RabbitMQ nodes and used to configure all aspects of the broker. Use it to configure an administration user in the broker, as follows:

```
$ sudo rabbitmqctl add_user cc-admin taxi123
Adding user "cc-admin" ...

$ sudo rabbitmqctl set_user_tags cc-admin administrator
Setting tags for user "cc-admin" to [administrator] ...
```

By default, RabbitMQ comes with a guest user that's authenticated with the guest password. Change this password to something else, as follows:

```
$ sudo rabbitmqctl change_password guest guest123
```

Navigating back to the management console login screen allows us to log in with the username `cc-admin` and the password `taxi123`.

The welcome screen provides an overview of the broker's internals, as shown in the following screenshot:

Fig 1.14: The main dashboard of the management console

Note that at this point, the `cc-admin` user is not able to examine any exchange or queue in any vhost. For now, another user must be created for development purposes so that applications can connect to RabbitMQ.

Create the `cc-dev` user, as follows:

```
$ sudo rabbitmqctl add_user cc-dev taxi123
Adding user "cc-dev" ...
```

As discussed earlier in this chapter, RabbitMQ supports the notion of vhosts, which is where different users can have different access privileges. The CC development environment will have a vhost, also known as vhost. Anything that happens in the vhost happens in isolation from any other environment created in the future (such as a QA environment). It is possible to set per-vhost limits on a number of queues and concurrent client connections in later versions of RabbitMQ (3.7+).

Create a vhost called `cc-dev-vhost`, as follows:

```
$ sudo rabbitmqctl add_vhost cc-dev-vhost
Adding vhost "cc-dev-vhost" ...
```

This creates a user and a vhost for development.

Configuring dedicated vhosts

RabbitMQ comes with a default vhost called / that the guest user has full permissions for. Though this is convenient for quick tests, it is recommended that a dedicated vhost is created to keep concerns separated so that it is possible to completely drop a vhost and restart from scratch without unexpected impacts.

As it stands, neither the `cc-admin` nor `cc-dev` users have permission to do anything on `cc-dev-vhost`. You can fix this by giving the vhost full rights, as follows:

```
$ sudo rabbitmqctl set_permissions -p cc-dev-vhost cc-admin ".*" ".*" ".*"
Setting permissions for user "cc-admin" in vhost "cc-dev-vhost" ... $ sudo
rabbitmqctl set_permissions -p cc-dev-vhost cc-dev ".*" ".*" ".*"
Setting permissions for user "cc-dev" in vhost "cc-dev-vhost" ...
```

To recap what was just done, most of the command is straightforward but the ".*" ".*" ".*" part looks a tad mysterious, so let's analyze it.

It is a triplet of permissions for the considered vhost, which grants **configure**, **write**, and **read** permissions on the designated resources for the considered user and vhost. Resources, which consist of exchanges and queues, are designated by regular expressions that match their names. In this case, any resource that's requested via the .* regular expression is allowed.

The actual commands that are granted depend on the resource type and the granted permissions. For a complete list of the access control policies supported by RabbitMQ, see `http://www.rabbitmq.com/access-control.html`.

As an alternative to all command lines, turn to the user management features of the management console. Click on the **Admin** tab of the console and then on the `cc-dev` user listed in the **Users** tab to view information similar to what's shown in the following screenshot. The entire user configuration that was set from the command line is visible and can be edited in the management console:

Fig 1.15: User management from the RabbitMQ management console

The details of an individual user can be found by clicking on a given user's name in the management console:

Fig 1.16: Details of an individual user in the management console

The RabbitMQ broker and the management plugin (Web UI) have been installed and the vhost and the users have been configured.

Summary

This chapter explored the architectural and design promises of messaging, including how AMQP and RabbitMQ deliver on these promises. In addition, the reason why the taxi agency Complete Car decided to introduce RabbitMQ in its software landscape was discovered. Finally, a RabbitMQ broker was installed and a user and various vhosts were configured for it. Armed with a basic understanding of message queues and RabbitMQ, the next chapter builds on these concepts and explores the architecture behind the Complete Car taxi application.

It's time to hit the ground running and write some code. Turn to the next chapter to start building a RabbitMQ-powered application!

2
Creating a Taxi Application

In everyday conversation, people greet each other, exchange banter, and then eventually end the conversation and continue on their way. Low-level TCP connections function in the same way over lightweight channels in RabbitMQ. Applications that are going to exchange messages over RabbitMQ need to establish a permanent connection to the message broker. When this connection is established, a channel needs to be created so that message-oriented interactions, such as publishing and consuming messages, can be performed.

After demonstrating these fundamentals, this chapter will cover how a broker uses **exchanges** to determine where each message should be delivered. An exchange is like a mailman: it delivers messages to their proper queues (mailboxes) for consumers to find at a later time.

The basic RabbitMQ concepts are shown in the following diagram:

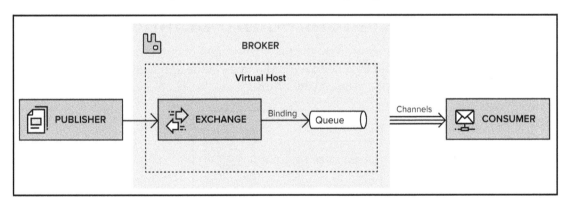

Fig 2.1: Basic RabbitMQ concepts

By the end of this chapter, you will have a solid understanding of the application architecture behind the **Complete Car** (**CC**) platform and how they sent the first message through RabbitMQ. This requires an introduction to two different types of exchanges: direct exchange, which delivers messages to a single queue, and topic exchange, which delivers messages to multiple queues based on pattern-matching routing keys.

To get the best start possible, following topics are covered:

- The application architecture behind CC
- Establishing a connection to RabbitMQ
- Sending the first messages
- Adding topic messages

Let's get started!

Technical requirements

The code files of this chapter can be found on GitHub at `https://github.com/ PacktPublishing/RabbitMQ-Essentials-Second-Edition/tree/master/Chapter02`.

The application architecture behind CC

CC needs one application that is used by the taxi drivers and one that is used by the customer. The customer should be able to request a taxi via the application, and the taxi driver should be able to accept a request (the ride):

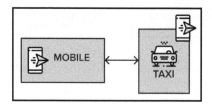

Fig 2.2: The customer requests a taxi via the CC application

The customer should be able to enter information about the starting point and the endpoint of the trip. Active drivers receive the requests and are able to accept them. The customer should, in the end, be able to follow the location of the taxi during the trip.

The following diagram shows the messaging architecture that CC wants to achieve:

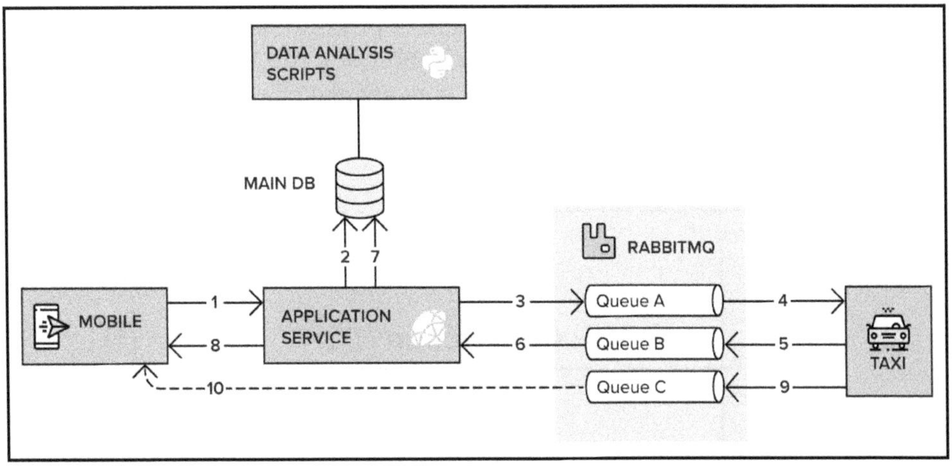

Fig 2.3: CC's main application architecture

This flow can be explained in 10 steps, as highlighted in the preceding diagram:

1. A customer uses CC's mobile application to book a taxi. A request is now sent from the mobile application to the Application Service. This request includes information about the trip that the customer wants to book.
2. The Application Service stores the request in a database.
3. The Application Service adds a message with information about the trip to a queue in RabbitMQ.
4. Connected taxi cars subscribe to the message (the booking request).
5. A taxi responds to the customer by sending a message back to RabbitMQ.
6. The Application Service subscribes to the messages.
7. Again, the Application Service stores the information in a database.
8. The Application Service forwards the information to the customer.
9. The taxi app starts to automatically send the taxi's geographical location at a given interval to RabbitMQ.
10. The location of the taxi is then passed straight to the customer's mobile application, via WebSockets, so that they know when the taxi arrives.

Let's begin by taking a closer look at *steps 1, 2, 3, and 4,* as shown in the preceding diagram, where a customer requests a taxi (a message is published to RabbitMQ) and a taxi driver receives the request (a message is consumed from RabbitMQ).

Establishing a solid connection to RabbitMQ

As mentioned in Chapter 1, *A Rabbit Springs to Life*, a physical network connection must be established between the application servers and RabbitMQ. An **Advanced Message Queuing Protocol** (**AMQP**) connection is a link between the client and the broker that performs underlying networking tasks, including initial authentication, IP resolution, and networking:

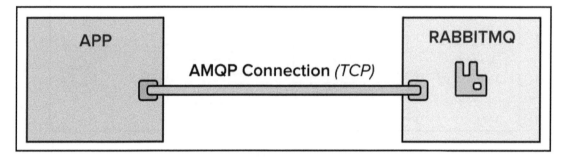

Fig 2.4: AMQP connection between the application and RabbitMQ

Each AMQP connection maintains a set of underlying channels. A channel reuses a connection, forgoing the need to reauthorize and open a new TCP stream, making it more resource-efficient.

The following diagram illustrates a channel within a connection between an application and RabbitMQ:

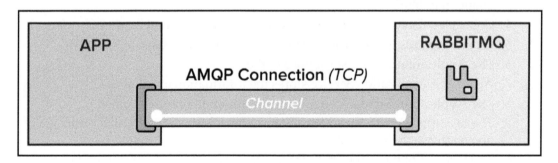

Fig 2.5: Channels allow you to use resources more efficiently

Unlike creating channels, creating connections is a costly operation, very much like it is with database connections. Typically, database connections are pooled, where each instance of the pool is used by a single execution thread. AMQP is different in the sense that a single connection can be used by many threads through many multiplexed channels.

The handshake process for an AMQP connection requires at least seven TCP packets, and even more when using TLS. Channels can be opened and closed more frequently if needed:

- AMQP connections: 7 TCP packages
- AMQP channel: 2 TCP packages
- AMQP publish: 1 TCP package (more for larger messages)
- AMQP close channel: 2 TCP packages
- AMQP close connection: 2 TCP packages
- Total 14-19 packages (plus Acks)

The following diagram illustrates an overview of the information that's sent to connections and channels:

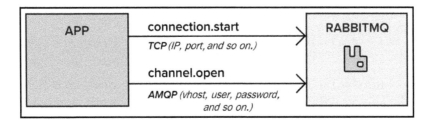

Fig 2.6: The handshake process for an AMQP connection

Establishing a single long-lived connection between the Application Service and RabbitMQ is a good start.

A decision must be made regarding which programming language and client library to use. The first few examples in this book are written in Ruby, and the client library Bunny (https://github.com/ruby-amqp/bunny) is used to publish and consume messages. Ruby is an easy language to read and understand, even if it is unfamiliar to you.

The application must be configured to use a certain connection endpoint, often referred to as a connection string; for example, a host and port. The connection string contains the information needed to be able to establish a connection. AMQP's assigned port number is 5672. TLS/SSL-encrypted AMQP can be used via AMQPS; it's a secure version of the AMQP protocol that's assigned port 5671.

The library is the element that opens the TCP connection to the target IP address and port. The connection parameters have been added as a URI string to an environment variable to the code called RABBITMQ_URI. There is no URI standard for AMQP URIs, but this format is widely used:

```
RABBITMQ_URI="amqp://user:password@host/vhost"
```

According to the Ruby (Bunny) documentation, connecting to RabbitMQ is simple. The code for this is divided into code blocks, and can be found later in this chapter:

1. Add the username, the password, and the `vhost` that were set up in `Chapter 1`, *A Rabbit Springs to Life*, and then add the string to an environment variable on the machine:

   ```
   RABBITMQ_URI="amqp://cc-dev:taxi123@localhost/cc-dev-vhost"
   ```

2. Require the `bunny` client library:

   ```
   # Require client library
   require "bunny"
   ```

3. Read the connection URI from the environment variable and start a connection:

   ```
   connection = Bunny.new ENV['RABBITMQ_URI']
   # Start a session with RabbitMQ
   connection.start
   ```

This seems straightforward so far, but CC requires production-grade code that can gracefully handle failures. What if RabbitMQ is not running? Clearly, it is bad if the whole application is down. What if RabbitMQ needs to be restarted? CC wants its application to recover gracefully if any issues occur. In fact, CC wants its application to keep functioning, regardless of whether the whole messaging subsystem is working or not. The user experience must be smooth and easy to understand, as well as reliable.

In summary, the behavior CC wishes to achieve is as follows:

- If the connection to RabbitMQ is lost, it should reconnect by itself.
- If the connection is down, sending or fetching messages should fail gracefully.

When the application connects to the broker, it needs to handle connection failures. No network is reliable all the time and misconfigurations and mistakes happen; the broker might be down, and so on. While not automatic, in this case, error detection should happen early in the process.

To handle TCP connection failures in Bunny, it is necessary to catch the exception:

```
begin
  connection = Bunny.new ENV['RABBITMQ_URI']
  connection.start
rescue Bunny::TCPConnectionFailed => e
  puts "Connection to server failed"
end
```

Detecting network connection failures is nearly useless if an application cannot recover from them. Recovery is an important part of error handling.

Some client libraries offer automatic connection recovery features that include consumer recovery. Any operation that's attempted on a closed channel will fail with an exception. If Bunny detects a TCP connection failure, it will try to reconnect every 5 seconds with no limit regarding the number of reconnection attempts. It is possible to disable automatic connection recovery by adding `automatic_recovery => false` to `Bunny.new`. This setting should only be used if you're reconnecting in some other way, or when testing the connection string.

> Messages can be sent across languages, platforms, and operating systems. You can choose from a number of different client libraries for different languages. There are lots of client libraries out there, but here are some that are recommended:
>
> - Python: Pika
> - Node.js: amqplib
> - PHP: php-amqplib
> - Java: amqp-client
> - Clojure: Langohr

This section has shown how CC manages to establish a connection to RabbitMQ. We demonstrated why a long-lived connection is recommended and how to handle some common errors. Now, it's time to create a channel inside the connection.

Working with channels

Every AMQP protocol-related operation occurs over a channel. The channel instances are created by the connection instance. As described, a channel is a virtual (AMQP) connection inside the (TCP) connection. All operations performed by a client happen on a channel, queues are declared on channels, and messages are sent over channels.

A channel never exists on its own; it's always in the context of a connection:

```
# Declare a channel
channel = connection.create_channel
```

Channels in a connection are closed once the connection is closed or when a channel error occurs. Client libraries allow us to observe and react to channel exceptions.

More **exceptions** are usually thrown at a channel level than at the connection level. Channel-level exceptions often indicate errors the application can recover from, such as, when it has no permissions, or when attempting to consume from a deleted queue. Any attempted operation on a closed channel will also fail with an exception.

 Even though channel instances are technically thread-safe, it is strongly recommended to avoid having several threads that are using the same channel concurrently.

CC is now able to connect to a RabbitMQ broker, open a channel, and issue a series of commands, all in a thread-safe and exception-safe manner. It's now time to build on this foundation!

Building the taxi request tool

Now, it's time to build the message flow.

First, the customer will send a simple HTTP request from the mobile application to the Application Service. This message will contain meta-information such as a timestamp, sender and receiver IDs, and the destination and requested taxi ID.

The message flow will look something like this:

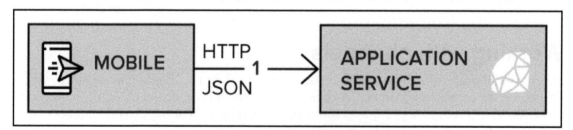

Fig 2.7: The frontend/backend interactions of CC's main application

The Application Service stores the information in a database so that all the data becomes visible for the data analysis scripts in a later state.

How the data is stored in the database is not handled in these examples since that's not the main case being followed in this chapter. The easiest method would be to allow the Application Service to add the information to the database. Another option is to offload the Application Service and put new messages into a message queue between the database and the Application Service and let another service subscribe to those messages and handle them; that is, store them in the database.

The flow between the mobile device, the Application Service, and RabbitMQ is illustrated in the following diagram:

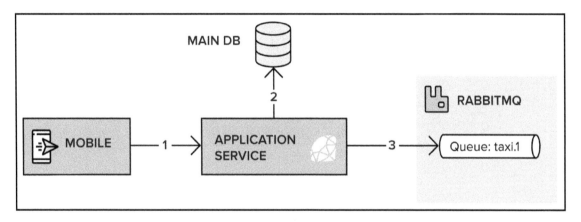

Fig 2.8: The flow between the mobile device, the Application Service, and RabbitMQ

Regarding our main flow, the discussion about AMQP in Chapter 1, *A Rabbit Springs to Life,* detailed how messages are published to exchanges after being routed to queues to be consumed.

A routing strategy determines which queue (or queues) the message will be routed to. The routing strategy bases its decision on a routing key (a free-form string) and potentially on message meta-information. Think of the routing key as an address that the exchange uses to decide how the message should be routed. It also needs to be a binding between an exchange and the queue to enable a message to flow from the former to the latter.

Now, let's explore the direct exchange.

The direct exchange

A direct exchange delivers messages to queues based on a message routing key. A message goes to the queue(s) whose bindings routine key matches the routing key of the message.

CC only has two cars, so it starts out with a simple communication system where one customer can request a taxi from one driver. In this case, one message needs to be routed to the queue acting as the inbox of that driver. Therefore, the exchange-routing strategy that will be used is a direct one, matching the destination queue name with the routing key used when the message is produced, as illustrated in the following diagram:

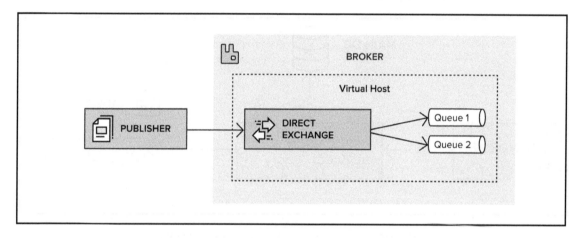

Fig 2.9: The direct exchange route messages to specific queues

An example use case of direct exchange could be as follows:

1. The customer orders the taxi named **taxi.1**. An HTTP request is sent from the customer's mobile application to the Application Service.
2. The Application Service sends a message to RabbitMQ with a routing key, **taxi.1**. The message routing key matches the name of the queue, so the message ends up in the **taxi.1** queue.

The following diagram demonstrates how the direct exchange message routing would happen:

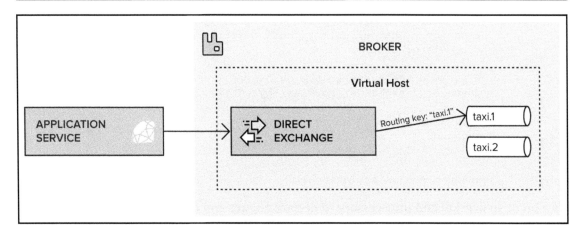

Fig 2.10: The direct exchange routing messages to specific queues based on the routing key

This may not be the most efficient approach to scale. In fact, it will be reviewed as soon as CC has more cars, but it's the easiest way to get started and launch the application fast.

Let's follow the first code CC creates as the initial application and learn about the different concepts at the same time. The code at the beginning of the code block has been taken from the connection and channel section:

1. Require the `bunny` client library.
2. Read the `URI` connection from the environment variable and start a connection.
3. Start a communication session with RabbitMQ.
4. Declare the `taxi.1` queue.
5. Declare the `taxi.1` direct exchange.
6. Bind the `taxi.1` queue to the `taxi-direct` exchange with the `taxi.1` routing key:

```
# 1. Require client library
require "bunny"

# 2. Read RABBITMQ_URI from ENV
connection = Bunny.new ENV["'RABBITMQ_URI"]

# 3. Start a communication session with RabbitMQ
connection.start
channel = connection.create_channel

def on_start(channel)
  # 4. Declare a queue for a given taxi
  queue = channel.queue("taxi.1", durable: true)
```

```
# 5. Declare a direct exchange, taxi-direct
exchange = channel.direct("taxi-direct", durable: true,
auto_delete: true)

# 6. Bind the queue to the exchange
queue.bind(exchange, routing_key: "taxi.1")

# 7. Return the exchange
exchange
end

exchange = on_start(channel)
```

It's a bit of an overkill and unnecessary to declare queues and exchanges for every message that's sent, so it's highly recommended to create a method that handles the setup of the application. This should be a method that creates the connection and declares queues, exchanges, and so on. The method in this example is simply called `on_start`, which declares the queue and binds an exchange to the queue.

If the exchange doesn't exist when something is published to it, it will raise exceptions. If the exchange already exists, it will do nothing; otherwise, it will actually create one. This is why it's safe to declare queues every time the application starts or before publishing a message.

Channels are killed by exceptions. In CC's case, sending to a nonexistent exchange would not only raise an exception, but it would also terminate the channel where the error occurred. Any subsequent code that tries to use the terminated channel will fail as well.

In addition to using the direct type, CC has configured the `durable` type, `autoDelete`, and the `argument` properties of the exchange. This exchange should not go away after a restart of RabbitMQ, nor when it's unused, which explains the values used in the configuration.

An exchange declaration is only idempotent if the exchange properties are the same. Trying to declare an already-existing exchange with different properties will fail. Always use consistent properties in an exchange declaration. If you're making a change to the properties, delete the exchange before declaring it with the new properties. The same rule applies to a queue declaration.

After creating the exchange, the taxi queue is created and bound to it.

The queue is declared with a similar approach to an exchange, but with slightly different properties, as follows:

- `durable`: True – the queue must stay declared, even after a broker restart.
- `autoDelete`: False – keep the queue, even if it's not being consumed anymore.
- `exclusive`: False – this queue should be able to be consumed by other connections (several application servers can be connected to RabbitMQ and accessed from different connections).
- `arguments`: Null – no need to custom configure the queue.

The queue is bound to the exchange using its own name as the routing key so that the direct routing strategy can route messages to it. When this is done, publishing messages to the `taxi-direct` exchange will actually deliver messages to the taxi queue whose name matches the published routing key.

 If no queue is bound to an exchange, or if the routing strategy can't find a matching destination queue, the message that was published to the exchange will be discarded silently. As an option, it is possible to be notified when unroutable messages are discarded, as shown in subsequent chapters.

Again, when the same properties are used, these operations are idempotent, so the queue can safely be declared and bound to the exchange, again and again

Although direct exchange has been covered in this chapter, AMQP 0-9-1 brokers provide four different types of exchanges. Depending on the binding setups you have between queues and parameters, these exchanges route messages differently. The upcoming chapters look closer at the other types of exchanges. For now, here is a short explanation of each:

- **Fanout**: Messages are routed to all queues bound to the fanout exchange.
- **Topic**: Wildcards must form a match between the routing key and the binding's specific routing pattern.
- **Headers**: Use the message header attributes for routing.

Now, it's time to send our first message to RabbitMQ!

Sending the first messages

The basic concept and initial setup has already been covered, so let's jump in and send the first messages!

First, let's take a look at the `order_taxi` method, which is in charge of sending messages for the initial car request:

```
def order_taxi(taxi, exchange)
  payload = "example-message"
  message_id = rand
 exchange.publish(payload,
    routing_key: taxi,
    content_type: "application/json",
    content_encoding: "UTF-8",
    persistent: true,
    message_id: message_id)
end

exchange = on_start(channel)
order_taxi("taxi.1", exchange)
```

`order_taxi` is going to be called every time a user wants to order a taxi. There is no guarantee that the addressee has ever logged into the system, so as far as the sender is concerned, it's impossible to be sure the destination queue exists. The safest path is to declare the queue on every message sent, bearing in mind that this declare operation is idempotent, so it will not do anything if the queue already exists. This may seem strange at first, but it's the sender's responsibility to ensure the addressee's queue exists if they want to be sure the message will not get lost.

This is a common pattern with AMQP when there is no strong **happens-before** relationship between events. **Re-declaration** is the way to go. Conversely, the **check-then-act** pattern is discouraged; trying to check the pre-existence of an exchange or a queue does not guarantee success in the typical distributed environment where AMQP is used.

The method for publishing a message is very simple; call `publish` toward the `exchange`. Then, use the queue name as the routing key (as per the **direct** routing) and an array of bytes that represent the actual message payload. It's possible to add some optional message properties, which could include the following:

- `content_type` (**string**): A message is published and consumed as a byte array, but nothing really says what these bytes represent. In the current situation, both publishers and consumers are in the same system, so it could be assumed that the content type is expected. That being said, always specify the content type so that messages are self-contained; whichever system ends up receiving or introspecting a message will know for sure what the byte array it contains represents.

- `content_encoding` (**string**): A specific encoding (UTF-8) is used when serializing string messages into byte arrays so that they can be published. Again, in order for the messages to be self-explicit, provide all the necessary meta-information to allow them to be read.

- `message_id` (**string**): As demonstrated later in this book, message identifiers are an important aspect of traceability in messaging and distributed applications. In the example is a random message id generated.

- `persistent` (**boolean**): Specifies if the message should be persisted to disk or not.

> Do not confuse exchange and queue durability with message persistence; non-persistent messages stored in a durable queue will be gone after a broker restart, leaving you with an empty queue.
>
> Additionally, persistent messages in a non-persistent queue will be gone after a broker restart, also leaving you with an empty queue.
>
> Ensure that messages are not lost by declaring a queue as **durable** and setting the message delivery mode to **persistent.**

But what would happen if sending the message fails, such as when the connection with RabbitMQ is broken?

Why would you ever use a non-persistent delivery mode? Isn't the whole point of a message broker such as RabbitMQ to guarantee that messages aren't lost? This is true, but there are circumstances where this guarantee can be relaxed. Consider a scenario where a publisher bombards the broker with a lot of non-critical messages. Using a non-persistent delivery here would mean that RabbitMQ wouldn't need to constantly access the disk, thus providing better performance in this case.

Before going any further, let's take a look at the structure of an AMQP message.

AMQP message structure

The following screenshot illustrates the structure of an AMQP message and includes the four AMQP message properties just used, plus a few new ones. Note that this diagram uses the specification name of the fields and that each language implementation renames them slightly so that they can be valid names. For example, `content-type` becomes `contentType` in Java, and `content_type` in Ruby:

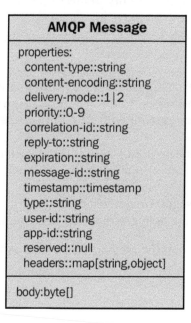

Fig 2.11: Properties of an AMQP message

Except for `reserved`, all these properties are free to use and, unless otherwise specified, are ignored by the AMQP broker. In the case of RabbitMQ, the only field that is supported by the broker is the `user-id` field, which is validated to ensure it matches the name of the broker user that established the connection. Notice how the `headers` property allows us to add extra key-value pairs in case none of the standard properties fit the requirements.

The next section explains how messages are consumed.

Consuming messages

Now, let's turn our attention to the method in charge of retrieving messages, which is *step 4* in the main architecture of CC, which can be found in the *The application architecture behind CC* section.

Here, the taxi application can check the queue for new messages at a regular interval. This is a so-called synchronous approach. This would mean holding the application thread in charge of dealing with the poll requests until all pending messages have been removed from the queue, as illustrated in the following diagram:

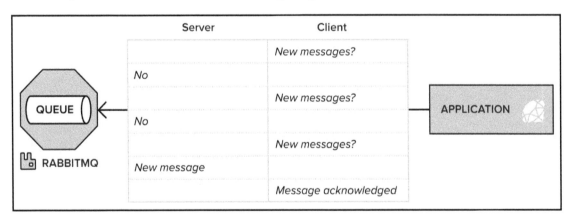

Fig 2.12: A client asking for new messages in the broker

A frontend regularly polling the backend for messages would soon start to take its toll in terms of load, meaning that the overall solution would begin to suffer from performance degradation.

Instead, CC wisely decides to build the solution in favor of a server-push approach. The idea is to server-push messages to the clients from the broker. Luckily, RabbitMQ offers two ways to receive messages: there's the polling-based `basic.get` method and the push-based `basic.consume` method. As illustrated in the following diagram, messages are pushed to the consumer:

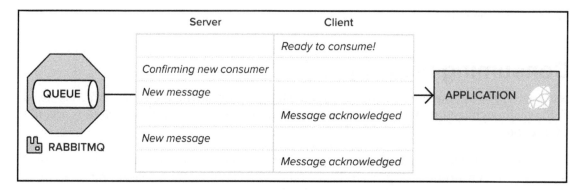

Fig 2.13: Consumer subscribing messages from the broker

The `subscribe` method adds a consumer to the queue, which then subscribes to receive message deliveries.

> Make sure that the consumer consumes messages from the queue instead of using basic GET actions. The `basic.get` command is comparatively expensive when it comes to resources.

With `subscribe`, the messages are delivered to the client from the broker when new messages are ready and the client has availability. This allows, in general, the smooth processing of messages. Additionally, using `subscribe` means that a consumer is connected as long as the channel it was declared on is available or until the client cancels it.

The message process is running smoothly and effortlessly, almost as if nothing is happening! That is, of course, until alerts are set in motion to acknowledge and/or negative acknowledge whether a part of the process has run as expected, or not as planned.

Acknowledgment and negative acknowledgment

RabbitMQ needs to know when a message can be considered **successful** in terms of being sent to the consumer as expected. The broker should then delete messages from the queue once the broker receives the response; otherwise, the queue would overflow. The client can reply to the broker by either acking (acknowledge) the message when it receives it or when the consumer has completely processed the message. In either situation, once the message has been ack:ed, it's removed from the queue.

Therefore, it's up to the consumer to acknowledge a message if and only if it is done with processing, or if it is certain that there is no risk of losing the message if it is processed asynchronously.

To avoid a situation where a message could be forever lost (for example, worker crashed, exceptions, and so on), the consuming application should not acknowledge a message until it is completely finished with it.

A message is rejected by an application when the application indicates to the broker that processing has failed or cannot be accomplished at the time. Nack, or negative-acknowledge, tells RabbitMQ that a message was not handled as instructed. Nack'ed messages, by default, are sent back to the queue for another try.

Acknowledges will be covered in detail in `Chapter 3`, *Sending Messages to Multiple Taxi Drivers.*

Ready? Set? Time to RUN, Rabbit!

Running the code

Now, it's time to set up some code for the consumer. You'll be able to recognize most of this code from the previous section, *Sending the first messages:*

1. Require client libraries.
2. Read `RABBITMQ_URI` from `ENV`.
3. Start a communication session with RabbitMQ.
4. Declare a queue for a given taxi.
5. Declare a direct exchange, `taxi-direct`.
6. Bind the queue to the exchange.
7. Subscribe to the queue.

What follows is the code that's required for the initial consumer setup:

```ruby
# example_consumer.rb
# 1. Require client library
require "bunny"

# 2. Read RABBITMQ_URI from ENV
connection = Bunny.new ENV["RABBITMQ_URI"]

# 3. Start a communication session with RabbitMQ
connection.start
channel = connection.create_channel

# Method for the processing
def process_order(info)

  puts "Handling taxi order"
  puts info
  sleep 5.0
  puts "Processing done"
end

def taxi_subscribe(channel, taxi)
  # 4. Declare a queue for a given taxi
  queue = channel.queue(taxi, durable: true)

  # 5. Declare a direct exchange, taxi-direct
  exchange = channel.direct("taxi-direct", durable: true, auto_delete:
true)

  # 6. Bind the queue to the exchange
  queue.bind(exchange, routing_key: taxi)

  # 7. Subscribe from the queue
  queue.subscribe(block: true, manual_ack: false) do |delivery_info,
properties, payload|
    process_order(payload)
  end
end

taxi = "taxi.1"
taxi_subscribe(channel, taxi)
```

Here, two flags were added to the `subscribe` method that need to be explained. Let's look at them in detail:

- `block` (Boolean, default `false`): Should the call block the calling thread? This option can be useful for keeping the main thread of a script alive. It is incompatible with automatic connection recovery and is not generally recommended.
- `manual_ack` (Boolean, default `false`): In CC's case, since the risk of losing a message is acceptable during this phase, the system does not manually acknowledge messages. Instead, it informs the broker to consider them as acknowledged as soon as it fetches them (more on manual acknowledgment later in this book).

And that's it! CC now has a working order request inbox ready to be tested. Next, we'll look at the management console when activated taxis are running.

Running the application

With the application running and a server connected to RabbitMQ, the following established connections can be seen from the management console:

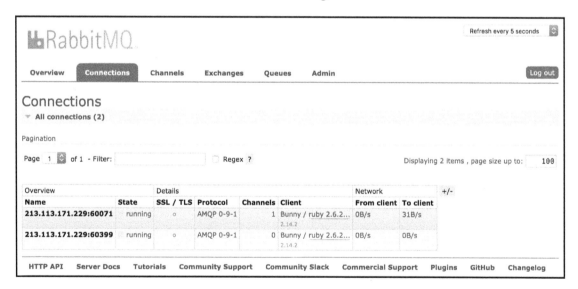

Fig 2.14: The management console provides connection information

Notice how the upstream and downstream network throughputs are clearly represented, and that the channels that get opened and closed very quickly are hard to see from the management console. So, let's look at the following exchanges:

Fig 2.15: The taxi-direct direct exchange showing up in the management console

The user exchange and the rate of messages coming in and out are shown in the management console. The fact that they are being consumed as fast as they come in is a good sign that the current architecture is sufficient for CC's needs and that messages are not piling up. But what are all these other exchanges that haven't been created by code and where are they coming from? The nameless exchange represented as (**AMQP default**) and all the exchanges with names that start with **amq.** are defined by the AMQP specification and, as such, must be provided by default by RabbitMQ. Now, what about queues? Let's have a look:

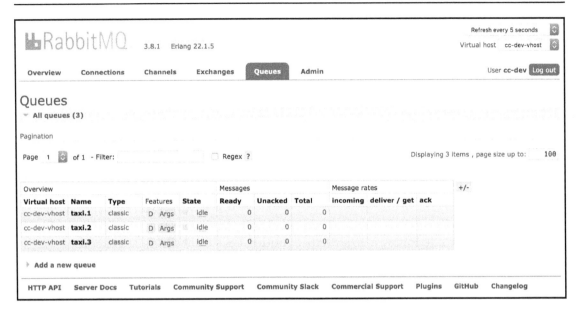

Fig 2.16: Each client-to-taxi inbox queue is visible in the management console

As expected, there is one queue per taxi and some nifty usage statistics. Notice how the **ack** column is empty, which is no surprise, given how message acknowledgment works. The queue is receiving messages while letting RabbitMQ know it won't be acknowledging them, so there is no activity related to acknowledging messages.

With enough RAM, RabbitMQ can deal with hundreds of queues and bindings without a problem, so multiple queues are not an issue.

Confident about its architecture and implementation, CC rolls out the client-to-taxi ordering subsystem. The client can send the request and the taxi can handle the request.

CC quickly expands the company with two new environmentally friendly cars. As in the previous solution, a client needs to send an order request message to a certain driver. Now, a new feature was requested – the capacity to send a message to a group of taxi cars. It should be possible for clients to select a normal taxi or an environmentally friendly taxi. Let's see how CC will implement this new feature through the power of RabbitMQ.

Adding topic messages

CC's application allows its taxis to organize themselves into groups by registering their topics of interest. The new feature to roll out will allow clients to send an order request to all taxis within a particular topic. It turns out that this feature matches a specific exchange routing rule, not surprisingly called topic! This type of exchange allows us to route the message to all the queues that have been bound with a routing key matching the routing key of the message. So, unlike the direct exchange that routes a message to one queue maximum, the topic exchange can route it to multiple queues. Two other examples of where topic-based routing could be applied are to location-specific data, such as traffic warning broadcasts, or to trip price updates.

A routing pattern consists of several words separated by dots. A best practice to follow is to structure routing keys from the most general element to the most specific one, such as `news.economy.usa` or `europe.sweden.stockholm`.
The topic exchange supports strict routing key matching and will also perform wildcard matching using * and # as placeholders for exactly one word and zero or more words, respectively.

The following diagram illustrates how the topic exchange will be used in CC's application. Notice how the single inbox queue remains unchanged and simply gets connected to the topic exchange via extra bindings, each of them reflecting the interest of a user:

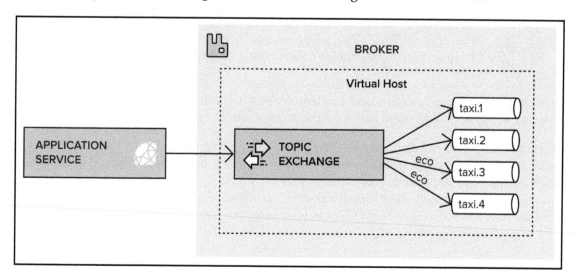

Fig 2.17: The topic exchange sending thematic messages to eco queues

Because the same inbox is used for everything, the code that's already in place for fetching messages doesn't need to be changed. In fact, this whole feature can be implemented with only a few additions. The first of these additions takes care of declaring the topic exchange in the existing `on_start` method, as follows:

```
def on_start(channel)
  # Declare and return the topic exchange, taxi-topic
  channel.topic("taxi-topic", durable: true, auto_delete: true)
end
```

There's nothing really new or fancy here; the main difference is that this exchange is called `taxi-topic` and is a `topic` type of exchange. Sending a message is even simpler than with the client-to-taxi feature because there is no attempt to create the addressee's queue. It wouldn't make sense for the sender to iterate through all the users to create and bind their queues, as only users already subscribed to the target topic at the time of sending will get the message, which is exactly the expected functionality. The `order_taxi` method is listed here:

```
# Publishing an order to the exchange
def order_taxi(type, exchange)
  payload = "example-message"
  message_id = rand
  exchange.publish(payload,
                   routing_key: type,
                   content_type: "application/json",
                   content_encoding: "UTF-8",
                   persistent: true,
                   message_id: message_id)
end

exchange = on_start(channel)
# Order will go to any eco taxi
order_taxi('taxi.eco', exchange)
# Order will go to any eco taxi
order_taxi('taxi.eco', exchange)
# Order will go to any taxi
order_taxi('taxi', exchange)
# Order will go to any taxi
order_taxi('taxi', exchange)
```

The difference is that, now, messages are published to the taxi-topic exchange. The rest of the code that creates and publishes the message is exactly the same as the client-to-taxi messaging. Lastly, information needs to be added when a new taxi subscribes or unsubscribes from certain topics:

```ruby
# example_consumer.rb

def taxi_topic_subscribe(channel, taxi, type)
  # Declare a queue for a given taxi
  queue = channel.queue(taxi, durable: true)

  # Declare a topic exchange
  exchange = channel.topic('taxi-topic', durable: true, auto_delete: true)

  # Bind the queue to the exchange
  queue.bind(exchange, routing_key: type)

  # Bind the queue to the exchange to make sure the taxi will get any order
  queue.bind(exchange, routing_key: 'taxi')

  # Subscribe from the queue
  queue.subscribe(block:true,manual_ack: false) do |delivery_info,
properties, payload|
    process_order(payload)
  end
end

taxi = "taxi.3"
taxi_topic_subscribe(channel, taxi, "taxi.eco.3")
```

taxi.3 is the new environmentally friendly taxi, now ready to receive orders from clients that want an environmentally friendly car.

The AMQP specification does not provide any means to introspect the current bindings of a queue, so it is not possible to iterate them and remove the ones not needed anymore in order to reflect a change in a taxi's topics of interest. This is not a terrible concern because the application is required to maintain this state anyway.

> The RabbitMQ management console exposes a REST API that can be used to perform queue binding introspection, among many other features not covered by the AMQP specification. More about that in upcoming chapters.

With this new code in place, everything works as expected. No code changes are needed to retrieve the new client-to-taxi orders because they arrive in the same inbox queue as the previous messages. Topical messages are sent and received correctly by the taxi cars, and all this happens with a minimal change and no increase in the number of queues. When connected to the management console, click on the **Exchanges** tab; the only visible difference is the new exchange topic; that is, `taxi-topic`.

Summary

This chapter covered how to connect to RabbitMQ and how to send and receive order messages. The car order system was successfully created, and direct and topic exchanges were put in motion in the context of CC's client-to-taxi and client-to-taxis features.

As Complete Car grows, so does the demand for new features in the taxi application. What's next for CC as it meets user demand? The next chapter explains how to work with channels and queues to expand the features of the app.

3
Sending Messages to Multiple Taxi Drivers

`Chapter 2`, *Creating a Taxi Application*, included information on how to connect to and consume messages from RabbitMQ. This chapter demonstrates setting the prefetch value, which specifies the number of messages being sent to the consumer at the same time. It also covers how consumers can either manually acknowledge messages or receive the messages without acknowledgment, the former allowing a zero-message loss design.

A new feature is requested of the **Complete Car** (**CC**) team, as the back office wants to be able to send information messages to all taxis at once. This is a prime opportunity to introduce the fanout exchange, which routes messages to all queues bound to them irrespective of the routing keys.

This chapter will cover the following topics:

- Working with channels and queues
- Specifying a consumer prefetch count
- Acknowledging messages
- Publishing to all queues

Technical requirements

The code files of this chapter can be found on GitHub at `https://github.com/ PacktPublishing/RabbitMQ-Essentials-Second-Edition/tree/master/Chapter03`.

Working with channels and queues

CC's drivers and customers are enjoying the **request taxi** feature that was rolled out in *Chapter 2, Creating a Taxi Application*. First, publishing messages to the direct exchange for customers ordering a single taxi was explained, and then instructions were given on implementing the topic exchange, which customers use when ordering a taxi with specific requirements. In both cases, the consumer is bound to the channel that was used to consume a particular queue. If this channel was closed, the consumer would stop receiving messages. Because a channel cannot be reopened and has to be recreated from scratch, both the channel and its consumption must be re-established if there are any problems.

Let's walk through some important points about consumers and queues in RabbitMQ:

- A queue can have multiple consumers (unless the exclusive tag is used).
- Each channel can have multiple consumers.
- Each consumer uses server resources, so it is best to make sure not to use too many consumers.
- Channels are full-duplex, meaning that one channel can be used to both publish and consume messages.

There is no logical limit to the number of channels or consumers a RabbitMQ broker can handle. There are, however, limiting factors, such as available memory, broker CPU power, and network bandwidth.

As each channel mobilizes memory and consumes CPU power, limiting the number of channels or consumers may be a consideration in some environments. The administrator can configure a maximum number of channels per connection by using the `channel_max` parameter.

It's now time to look into how to get as much out of the consumers as possible by setting a prefetch count.

Specifying a consumer prefetch count

The number of messages sent to the consumer at the same time can be specified through the **prefetch** count value. The prefetch count value is used to get as much out of the consumers as possible.

If the prefetch count is too small, it could negatively affect the performance of RabbitMQ, since the platform is usually waiting for permission to send more messages. The following diagram shows an example of a long idle time. The example has the prefetch set to one, meaning that RabbitMQ will not send the next message until after the delivery, processing, and acknowledgment of the message is complete.

In the example, the processing time is only 5 ms, with a round-trip time of 125 ms (60 ms + 60 ms + 5 ms):

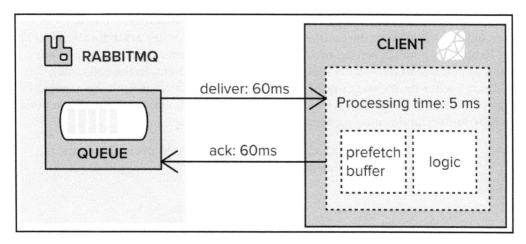

Fig 3.1: Round-trip time is 125 ms with a processing time of only 5 ms

A large prefetch count makes RabbitMQ send many messages from one queue to one consumer. If all messages are sent to a single consumer, it may be overwhelmed and leave the other consumers idle. The following diagram shows the consumer as they receive lots of messages while the other consumer is idle:

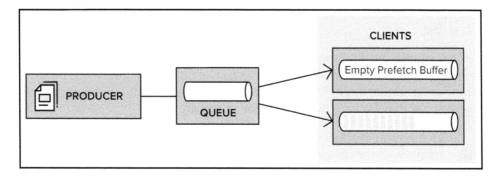

Fig 3.2: Consumer in an idling state

In *Chapter 2, Creating a Taxi Application*, a connection, channel, and consumer were created in Ruby. The following code block shows how to configure a prefetch value in Ruby:

```ruby
require "bunny"
connection = Bunny.new ENV["RABBITMQ_URI"]

connection.start
channel = connection.create_channel
channel.prefetch(1)
```

Note that the example shows the prefetch value at one `(1)`. This means that just one message will be delivered to the consumer until the consumer has **ack:ed/nack:ed** it. The default RabbitMQ prefetch setting provides an unlimited buffer for sending as many messages as possible to consumers that are ready to accept them. In the consumer, the client library caches the messages until processed. Prefetch settings limit the number of messages the client is able to receive before acknowledging them, rendering them invisible to other consumers, and removing them from the queue.

RabbitMQ supports channel-level, message-based prefetch counts, not connection or byte size-based prefetching.

Next, we'll look at how to set the correct prefetch value.

Setting the correct prefetch value

In a scenario of one or a few consumers who are quickly processing messages, it is recommended to prefetch many messages at once to keep the client as busy as possible. It is possible to divide the total round-trip time by the processing time for each message to get an estimated prefetch value – if the processing time stays the same and the network behavior is stable.

A low prefetch value is recommended in situations where there are many consumers and a short processing time. If the prefetch value is set too low, the consumers will be idle much of the time, waiting for messages to arrive. On the other hand, if the prefetch value is too high, one consumer may be very busy while the others are idle.

One typical mistake is to allow unlimited prefetch where one client receives all the messages, leading to high memory consumption and crashes, which cause all messages to be re-delivered.

In scenarios where there are many consumers and/or a longer time to process messages, it is recommended that the prefetch value is set to one (1) to evenly distribute messages among all consumers.

> If the client is set to auto-ack messages, prefetch settings will have no effect.

As mentioned in `Chapter 2`, *Creating a Taxi Application*, a consumer can acknowledge message delivery back to the broker. It's now time to look into how that can be done.

Acknowledging messages

A message that is in transit between the broker and the consumer might get lost in the event of a connection failure, and important messages probably need to be retransmitted. Acknowledgments let the server and clients know when to retransmit messages.

There are two possible ways to acknowledge message delivery – once a consumer receives the message (an automatic acknowledgment, auto-ack), and when a consumer sends back an acknowledgment (explicit/manual acknowledge). With auto-ack, the message is acknowledged as soon as it leaves the queue (and is thereby removed from the queue). It is best to auto-ack when high message speeds are required, if the connections are reliable, and if lost messages aren't a concern.

> Using manual acknowledgments on messages can have a performance impact on the system, compared to an automatic acknowledgment. If aiming for fast throughput, manual acknowledgments should be disabled, and auto acknowledgments should be used instead.

In CC's case, the risk of losing a message is not acceptable, so the preceding code has been changed to set the acknowledgment to `manual`, making it possible to determine when to acknowledge the message:

```
queue.subscribe(block: true, manual_ack: true)
```

The message also has to be acknowledged once it has been fully processed:

```
channel.acknowledge(delivery_info.delivery_tag, false)
```

As demonstrated, the method to manually acknowledge takes two arguments – the first is `delivery tag`, and the second is needed in case more than one message must be acknowledged at once. A delivery tag is a channel-specific number that the server uses to identify deliveries. It is of crucial importance that the consumer acknowledges the messages on the same channel as they were received because not doing so will raise an error.

After changing the code and running the application, the ack column rate is shown as non-zero. This is because manual acknowledgment is now used and the RabbitMQ client now sends ack messages over the wire to the broker. This has a cost in terms of bandwidth usage and general performance; however, if the priority is the guarantee of successful message processing over speed, it is perfectly acceptable.

 Use manual acknowledgment if there is a risk that the processing of a message may fail and the broker needs to eventually redeliver it. Redelivery of unacknowledged messages doesn't happen immediately unless the message is rejected or the channel is closed.

CC's journey with RabbitMQ is getting more exciting, causing the team to request a new feature to send important information to all taxi drivers directly. Let's see how to implement this new feature!

Publishing to all queues

With the new feature request in hand, the CC programming team came up with the new overall messaging architecture shown in the following diagram. The back-office application will be connected to RabbitMQ in order to publish information messages to all taxi drivers:

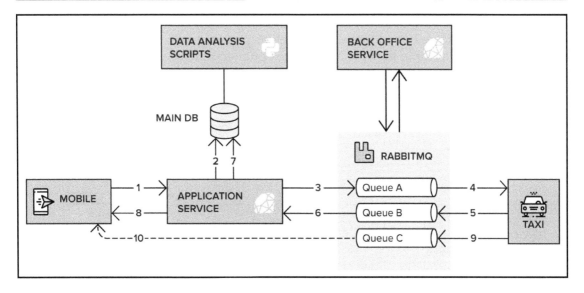

Fig 3.3: Back-office application in the architecture

To roll this out, one way could be to use the topic messaging that's already in place and create a special topic to which all drivers would be subscribed. However, there is an even cleaner and simpler approach offered by the AMQP protocol – fanout exchange.

Fanout exchange

Fanout exchange takes all messages that are coming in and delivers them to all queues that are bound to it. An easy-to-understand example of where to use a fanout is when messages need to be spread between many participants, like in a chat (however, there are probably better choices for pure chat applications).

Other examples include the following:

- Score board or leaderboard updates from sports news to mobile clients, or other global events
- Broadcasting various state and configuration updates in distributed systems

As shown in the following diagram, the fanout exchange routes a copy of each message it receives to all the queues bound to it. This model fits perfectly with the public address behavior that CC aims for in the new feature, the option to send a single message to all drivers:

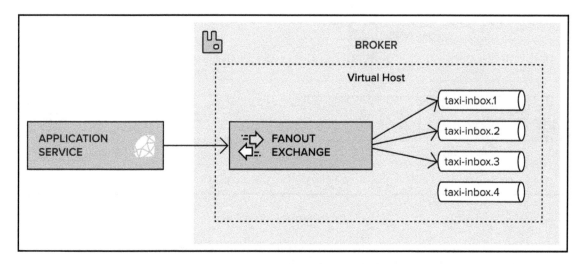

Fig 3.4: The fanout exchange routes to all bound queues

It's time to add the fanout exchange into CC's application.

Binding to the fanout

The back office should be able to publish a single message to all taxi drivers. This message could include current traffic information or information about a party that will happen during the evening. Because this new broadcast system will be infrequently used, the CC team was not as concerned about efficient connection management as they were with the main application. In fact, it's fine to connect and disconnect for each interaction with the fanout exchange because, in the case of temporary issues with the RabbitMQ broker, retries from the back office application will eventually succeed.

To start using the new fanout exchange in the back office, two steps must be performed: first, declare the fanout exchange when the application starts, and then bind the queue to it when a user logs in.

Number five in the following example shows the code added to the back office service in order to publish messages on this new exchange:

```
# 1. Require client library
require "bunny"

# 2. Read RABBITMQ_URI from ENV
connection = Bunny.new ENV["RABBITMQ_URI"]

# 3. Communication session with RabbitMQ
connection.start
channel = connection.create_channel

# 4. Declare queues for taxis
queue1 = channel.queue("taxi-inbox.1", durable: true)

queue2 = channel.queue("taxi-inbox.2", durable: true)

# 5. Declare a fanout exchange
exchange = channel.fanout("taxi-fanout")

# 6. Bind the queue
queue1.bind(exchange, routing_key: "")
queue2.bind(exchange, routing_key: "")

# 7. Publish a message
exchange.publish("Hello everybody! This is an information message from the
crew!", key: "")

# 8. Close the connection
connection.close
```

The logic in this code should feel familiar. An empty string is used as the routing key when binding the queue. The value doesn't really matter because the fanout exchange doesn't care about routing keys.

Notice that `exchange` is declared right before using it. This avoids relying on the implicit pre-existence of the exchange. Not doing that would mean that the main application would have to run once to create the exchange before the back office service can use it. Since the exchange declaration is idempotent, it can and should be declared at all times.

 Be particularly careful with AMQP client libraries that may use different default values for exchange and queue parameters; it's better to be explicit and to specify all values.

The same queues as in the direct and topic exchange example are not used since the taxi inbox queue only includes information messages. Two new queues (`taxi-inbox.1` and `taxi-inbox.2`) are instead declared and bounded to the exchange.

> Unless there is a strong guarantee that an exchange or a queue will pre-exist, assume it doesn't exist and declare it. It is better to be safe than sorry, especially when AMQP encourages it and provides the necessary means to do so.

With this code in place, the back office application can now send public information messages to all drivers. This is a great success, one that again reinforces CC in its decision to deploy RabbitMQ and build on it. Now, let's run the application.

Running the application

There's nothing spectacular to note when running the application; messages from the back office successfully flow to the drivers' inbox queues and the only visible change is the newly created driver fanout exchange.

This is visible in the management console shown in the following screenshot:

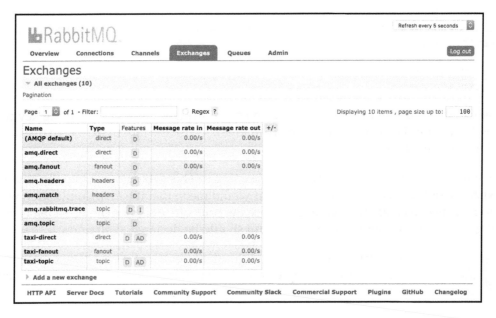

Fig 3.5: The fanout exchange for user queues is visible in the management console

At this point, it is interesting to take a look at the bindings of any particular queue. To do this, click on the **Queues** tab and then scroll down and click on **Bindings** to display the hidden window.

This will show what is reproduced, as in the following screenshot where each queue has multiple bindings – one for the user-to-taxi messaging feature, one for the topics messages, and a final one for the public address fanout feature:

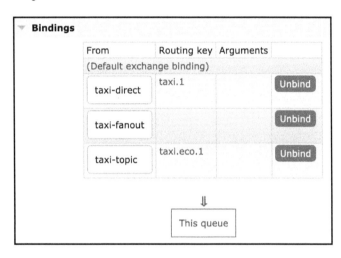

Fig 3.6: Each taxi queue has multiple bindings

Before concluding, let's pause for a second and relish the fact that there is now a successful taxi request integration that works across platforms. This may not seem important to anyone with a little experience in messaging systems; however, it is nothing short of a small miracle. Thanks to AMQP and RabbitMQ, the message broker can be replaced with any other AMQP-based message broker, and more services can be added in any chosen language.

Summary

This chapter talked about prefetch and manual acknowledgment from the consumer. The fanout exchange was introduced, to be able to broadcast a single message to all active queues. Up next, CC has new plans for its RabbitMQ system – they want to be able to clean up old messages in a smooth way and tweak the message delivery. They also want to be able to send messages to individual drivers from the back office service.

Continue on to the next chapter to find out what CC is up to!

4
Tweaking Message Delivery

What happens to messages that end up stuck in queues? Do they just disappear? What is the best way to prevent messages from being dropped silently, without warning? In this chapter, we will answers these questions thoroughly, looking in detail at message **time to live** (**TTL**) and dead-letter exchanges and queues. This chapter will also cover how the broker should react if a message cannot be routed to a specific queue using a mandatory flag. Additionally, the chapter will explain policies and the default exchange.

Expect to learn important information about the following topics:

- Handling dead letters
- Making delivery mandatory

Technical requirements

The code files of this chapter can be found on GitHub at `https://github.com/PacktPublishing/RabbitMQ-Essentials-Second-Edition/tree/master/Chapter04`.

Handling dead letters

Things are going very well at **Complete Car** (**CC**). The driver-information message feature is gaining traction as more and more drivers join the company. After a few months of activity, one thing becomes clear: not all taxi drivers log in to the application every day, which leads to messages piling up in taxi inbox queues.

Though the amount of data is not detrimental to the system, the idea of having messages lying around in queues, potentially forever, is not satisfactory. Imagine a taxi driver logging in after a couple of weeks of vacation and being flooded with obsolete messages—this is the negative type of user experience that CC is keen to avoid.

CC decides to address this by specifying a new rule: after one week, any message that is not delivered will be dealt with in one of two ways:

- It will be emailed to the user if it's an important information message.
- It will be discarded if it's an information message concerning the current traffic situation or other important information:

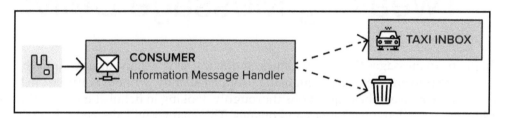

Fig 4.1: Email important information messages, discard other messages

The developers look at what is offered in terms of message expiration in RabbitMQ and list the following possible options that can be implemented:

- Standard AMQP message expiration property for published messages
- Custom RabbitMQ extension that allows users to define a message TTL per queue
- Custom RabbitMQ extension that allows users to define a TTL for the queue itself

The first option is interesting because it is a standard AMQP option; however, after reading more about how it is supported in RabbitMQ, it turns out that these messages are only discarded when the message reaches the head, or beginning, of a queue. Even if they have expired, the messages would still sit in the queue, which would defeat the purpose of what they're trying to achieve. CC rules out the last option as well, as they do not want the queue to be deleted. This leaves us with the second option of configuring each taxi inbox queue with a TTL that is enforced by RabbitMQ whether the queue is being consumed or not.

This is all fine and dandy, but what actually happens to messages when they expire? CC wants to consume these important messages in order to email them. So how do we achieve this? This is where RabbitMQ's **dead letter exchange** (**DLX**) comes in handy.

A dead letter is a message that can't be delivered, either because the intended target cannot be accessed or because it has expired. In the case of CC, messages that reach their TTL will become dead letters.

RabbitMQ offers the option to automatically route these dead letters to a specific exchange, a so-called DLX. Since CC wants to receive messages sent to this exchange, they must bind a queue to it, consume it, and take care of received messages. This queue acts as a **dead letter queue** (**DLQ**), the ultimate destination for dead messages.

The following diagram illustrates the overall DLX architecture that CC intends to roll out:

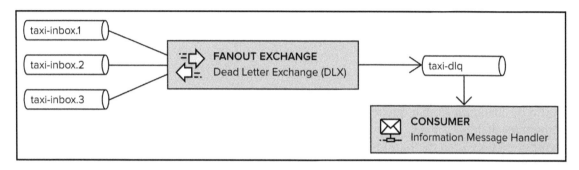

Fig 4.2: Dead-letter-handling architecture

A message that reaches its TTL is rerouted via the dead letter exchange to the **taxi-dlx** queue and finally handled by the consumer.

Note that when messages expire, they are published to the DLX using the original routing key they had when they were delivered to their taxi inbox queue. This behavior can be modified as RabbitMQ allows the definition of a specific routing key to use when messages are published to the DLX. The default suits CC, as the original routing key is an interesting bit of information they will use to find out the ID of the taxi. Therefore, the DLX exchange is constructed as a fanout in order to have all messages routed in the DLQ, whatever their original routing key may have been.

The battle plan is ready. It's now time to roll it out!

Refactoring queues

The first step in rolling out this architecture consists of configuring the taxi queues with the desired TTL of one week and a dead letter exchange equal to `taxi-dlx`.

By using the RabbitMQ extensions to AMQP, this can be achieved by respectively defining the `'x-message-ttl'` and `"x-dead-letter-exchange"` arguments when declaring the queue. Messages published to a queue that expires after the TTL are rerouted to the exchange with the given `x-dead-letter-routing-key`.

It's tempting to jump right to the code editor and modify the Ruby code written in `Chapter 3`, *Sending Messages to Multiple Taxi Drivers*, by using the following arguments:

```
# Declare a queue for a taxi inbox 1
queue1 = channel.queue('taxi-inbox.1',
  durable: true,
  arguments:{
    'x-message-ttl'=> 604800000,
    'x-dead-letter-exchange'=> 'taxi-dlx',
    'x-dead-letter-routing-key'=> 'taxi-inbox.1'
  }
)
```

However, this would be wrong on several levels. The main issue is that the declaration would be changing from a queue with no arguments to one with three arguments. Remember that in `Chapter 2`, *Creating a Taxi Application*, queue (or exchange) declaration is idempotent only if all the parameters that are used are the same. Any discrepancy in the declaration yields an exception and will be punished with an immediate channel termination.

> Make it a habit to double-check that the same attributes/parameters are always used when declaring existing queues and exchanges. Any difference will cause errors and terminate channels.

The other problem is that this change will only apply when taxi drivers log in. This is when the taxi queue is declared; however, it would not fulfill the requirement to apply the expiration rule to all existing queues independent of user actions. Finally, another thing to consider is that if these properties were configured at the queue declaration level, any change to one of them would require us to delete and recreate all of the queues. Clearly, the TTL and DLX configurations are cross-cutting concerns and should be configured in a more global fashion. Is that even possible?

The answer is yes! RabbitMQ has a simple and elegant solution to this problem in the concept of policies. RabbitMQ supports policies that define specific behaviors, and these policies can be applied to queues or exchanges. Policies are applied not only when a queue or exchange is declared, but also to an existing queue or exchange.

Both the queue message TTL and dead letter exchange are configurable via policies, but only a single policy can apply to a queue or exchange. Therefore, CC will craft a policy that combines both the TTL and DLX settings and apply it to all taxi inbox queues. This cannot be achieved via the AMQP protocol or by using the RabbitMQ client. Instead, the powerful command-line tools provided by RabbitMQ are the best way to achieve the policies needed.

This strategy to refactor the existing queues is achieved with the following single command-line operation:

```
$ sudo rabbitmqctl set_policy -p cc-dev-vhost Q_TTL_DLX "taxi\.\d+"
'{"message-ttl":604800000, "dead-letter-exchange":"taxi-dlx"}'
--apply-to queues
```

Let's take some time to dissect the preceding command:

- `sudo rabbitmqctl set_policy`: This part of the command uses the `set_policy` control command.
- `-p cc-dev-vhost`: This part of the command applies the message to the development virtual host.
- `Q_TTL_DLX`: This part of the command names the policy to make it obvious that it pertains to queue TTL and dead letter exchange.
- `"taxi\.\d+"`: This part of the command uses some regex to apply the entire command to the taxi queues only by selecting them by name.
- `'{"message-ttl":604800000, "dead-letter-exchange":"taxi-dlx"}'`: This part of the command uses a policy definition composed of a TTL of seven days in milliseconds and the name of the DLX.
- `--apply-to queues`: This part of the command ensures that this policy is only applied to queues, which is somewhat redundant with the regex, but acts as a safety net because it selects RabbitMQ entities by type instead of name.

Ready to run this command? Not so fast—the `"taxi-dlx"` exchange must be created and bound to the `"taxi-dlq"` queue. Applying this policy right now means that there will be seven days available to roll out the missing exchange and queue. Sure, this is plenty of time, but smart developers don't like to work against the clock if they can avoid it.

Instead of running the command right now, take the time to create the infrastructure in charge of dealing with the dead letters and roll it out to the application before applying the `"Q_TTL_DLX"` policy.

The policies are now set up, and it's time to add some code for the missing exchanges and queues.

Undertaking messages

The necessary infrastructure must be created to deal with expired messages. The dead letter queue needs to be declared, as well as the new dead letter fanout exchange. These need to be bound to each other.

The following needs to be done:

- Declare the `taxi-dlq` queue.
- Declare the `taxi-dlx` fanout exchange.
- Bind the `taxi-dlq` to the `taxi-dlx` fanout.
- Create a subscriber of the `taxi-dlq` queue that consumes and emails the dead letters.

To implement this behavior, simply add the exchange and queue with the following code to create the exchange and bind the queue to it:

1. Start by declaring two queues with `x-message-ttl` set to `604800000`:

```
queue1 = channel.queue('taxi-inbox.1', durable: true,
  arguments: {'x-message-ttl'=> 604800000, 'x-dead-letter-
exchange'=> 'taxi-dlx'})

queue2 = channel.queue('taxi-inbox.2', durable: true,
  arguments: {'x-message-ttl'=> 604800000, 'x-dead-letter-
exchange'=> 'taxi-dlx'})
```

2. Declare a fanout exchange `taxi-fanout`:

```
exchange = channel.fanout('taxi-fanout')
```

3. Bind both queues to the exchange:

```
queue1.bind(exchange, routing_key: "")
queue2.bind(exchange, routing_key: "")
```

4. Declare a dead letter queue, `taxi-dlq`:

```
taxi_dlq = channel.queue('taxi-dlq', durable: true)
```

5. Declare a dead letter fanout exchange, `taxi-dlx`:

```
dlx_exchange = channel.fanout('taxi-dlx')
```

6. Now `taxi-dlx` needs to be bound to `taxi-dlq`:

```
taxi_dlq.bind(dlx_exchange, routing_key: "")
```

7. Finally, publish a message:

```
exchange.publish("Hello! This is an information message!", key: "")
```

As you can see, this is just a standard fanout exchange declaration along with the related queue declaration and binding. The same logic was used when implementing the public address system in `Chapter 3`, *Sending Messages to Multiple Drivers*.

To simplify things even more, make sure that you log enough contextual data when an exception occurs. Always consider what information will be needed to perform forensics for a particular exception, if necessary.

After rolling out this code to the application servers, note that the dead letter exchange and queue have been correctly created. Now it is time to set the "`Q_TTL_DLX`" policy, as shown in the following code:

```
$ sudo rabbitmqctl set_policy
-p cc-dev-vhost Q_TTL_DLX "taxi-inbox\.\d+ " '{"message-ttl":604800000,
"dead-letter-exchange":"taxi-dlx"}' --apply-to queues

Setting policy "Q_TTL_DLX" for pattern "taxi-inbox\.\d+ " to "{\"message-
ttl\":604800000, \"dead-letter-exchange\":\"taxi-dlx\"}" with priority "0"
...
...done.
```

After running this script, use the management console to see what's been changed on the user inbox queue definitions.

The following screenshot shows a few of these queues:

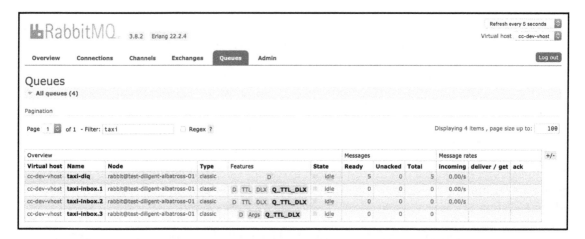

Fig 4.3: The Q_TTL_DLX policy is applied to all taxi queues

The following screenshot demonstrates that the **Q_TTL_DLX** policy has been applied to the taxi queue, while other queues, such as `taxi-dlq`, haven't been affected:

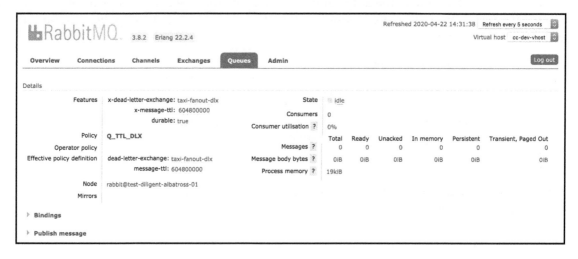

Fig 4.4: The Q_TTL_DLX policy is applied to the taxi-inbox.1 queue

In the management interface, click on the **Admin** tab and then the **Policies** tab (on the right). Note how the custom policy is visible in the following screenshot:

Fig 4.5: The Q_TTL_DLX policy is in the admin view

At this point, any message created that will stay for more than 7 days in a taxi queue will be unmercifully moved to the `taxi_dlq`, consumed, potentially emailed, and buried for real! But what should be done with the existing messages that were created before the policy was rolled out?

There is, unfortunately, no out-of-the-box solution to this problem, so the somewhat drastic measure to purge all the queues that are not empty and have no active subscribers must be taken. This is rough, but it is the only way to get out of the current situation. Moreover, it's a solution that is easily implemented with a simple script.

Thus far, the `rabbitmqctl` script has been used to manage the RabbitMQ broker. The next steps require the installation of a new script that comes bundled with the management console installed in Chapter 1, *A Rabbit Springs to Life*. This script, called `rabbitmqadmin`, can be downloaded by simply browsing to a particular URL in the management interface, namely `http://localhost:15672/cli/`. After following the displayed download instructions, install the script in a location that makes it available to all users (typically `/usr/local/bin` on a Linux machine).

More information on the `rabbitmqadmin` script can be found at `http://www.rabbitmq.com/management-cli.html`.

The following code shows how to create a script that will drop all consumerless queues that are not empty:

```bash
#!/bin/bash

queues_to_purge=`rabbitmqctl list_queues -p cc-dev-vhost name
messages_ready consumers | grep
"taxi\.[[:digit:]]\+[[:space:]]\+[1-9][[:digit:]]*[[:space:]]\+0" | awk '{
print $1}'`

for queue in $queues_to_purge ; do
    echo -n "Purging $queue ... "
    rabbitmqadmin -V cc-dev-vhost -u cc-admin -p taxi123 purge queue
name=$queue
done
```

Note that both `rabbitmqctl` and `rabbitmqadmin` were used to achieve the goal, the former with the ability to list specific attributes of queues in a way that's easy to parse and the latter with the ability to purge queues. After executing this script as a superuser, the state of the RabbitMQ broker is fit for purpose and the TTL and DLX policies will keep it that way in the long run!

CC now wants to send out a survey to all customers that have completed a ride with the taxi a few minutes after the completed ride. Let's see how it is possible to use dead letter exchanges and TTL to delay message delivery within RabbitMQ.

Delayed messages with RabbitMQ

While finishing off the work with this feature, the back office realizes that they can publish messages with a fixed delay so that consumers don't see them immediately. This is a perfect feature for their survey, which should be sent out to customers 5 minutes after a finished ride. The AMQP protocol doesn't have a native delayed queue feature, but one can easily be emulated by combining the message TTL function and the dead-lettering function.

The Delayed Message Plugin is available for RabbitMQ 3.5.3 and later versions of RabbitMQ. The Delayed Message Plugin adds a new exchange type to RabbitMQ. It is possible to delay messages routed via that exchange by adding a delay header to a message. You can read more about the plugin at `https://github.com/rabbitmq/rabbitmq-delayed-message-exchange`.

CC decides to publish survey request messages to a delayed queue once the driver has marked a ride as completed. All survey request messages are set to expire after a TTL of 5 minutes. The routing key of the message is then changed to the same as the destination queue name. This means that the survey request message will end up in the queue from which the survey request should be sent.

The following is an example of the code that CC would use. Messages are first delivered to the DELAYED_QUEUE called `work.later`. After 300,000 ms, messages are dead lettered and routed to the DESTINATION_QUEUE called `work.now`:

1. We start by assigning the variables:

   ```
   DELAYED_QUEUE='work.later'
   DESTINATION_QUEUE='work.now'
   ```

2. After that, we define the publish method. There are a lot of things happening here:

   - First, the delayed queue, DELAYED_QUEUE, is declared and `x-dead-letter-exchange` is set to the default queue.
   - A routing key for dead-lettering messages is set via the `x-dead-letter-routing-key` argument to DESTINATION_QUEUE.
   - The number of milliseconds to delay a message is specified in the message TTL `x-message-ttl` argument.

3. Finally, a message is published to the default exchange, where DELAYED_QUEUE is used as a routing key:

   ```
   def publish
     channel = connection.create_channel
     channel.queue(DELAYED_QUEUE, arguments: {
       'x-dead-letter-exchange' => '',
       'x-dead-letter-routing-key' => DESTINATION_QUEUE,
       'x-message-ttl' => 300000
     })
   ```

```
      channel.default_exchange.publish 'message content', routing_key:
DELAYED_QUEUE
        puts "#{Time.now}: Published the message"
        channel.close
    end
```

4. Then we define the subscribe method and handle the message:

```
def subscribe
  channel = connection.create_channel
  q = channel.queue DESTINATION_QUEUE, durable: true
  q.subscribe do |delivery, headers, body|
    puts "#{Time.now}: Got the message"
  end
end
```

5. Lastly, we call both methods:

```
subscribe()
publish()
```

That's it! The survey request feature is implemented. But, of course, a new feature is requested immediately. The back office wants to be able to send messages to single drivers and to also make sure that all drivers, even drivers without a RabbitMQ taxi inbox, receive the message. Let's look at the mandatory delivery of messages in RabbitMQ.

Making delivery mandatory

So far, the back office team at CC has been relying only on emails to interact with *individual* drivers. CC recently added the RabbitMQ-powered system discussed in Chapter 3, *Sending Messages to Multiple Taxi Drivers*, allowing the back office to send information messages to all drivers. They now want to explore the possibility of sending messages to individual drivers from the back office service. Furthermore, if possible, CC would like drivers who do not have an inbox queue set up on RabbitMQ to get the message emailed to them immediately.

In terms of messaging architecture, this is a known territory—the exact same model was put in place in Chapter 2, *Creating a Taxi Application*, for client-to-taxi messages, as illustrated in the following diagram:

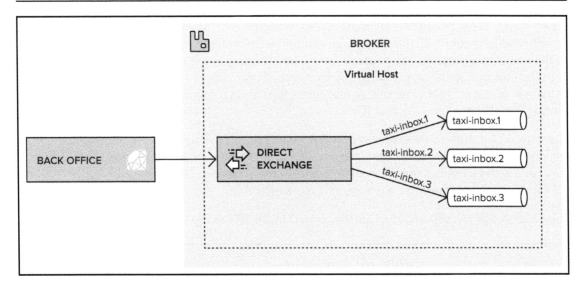

Fig 4.6: The back office team will use the taxi direct exchange for direct messages to drivers

A direct exchange is used. The only difference is that, unlike the main application, the back office will not create and bind a taxi queue prior to sending a message. Instead, the back office will have to somehow detect that no such queue exists already and revert to email delivery for the message.

What's unclear is how to achieve the second part of these requirements: how can the back office check for the existence of a queue? The AMQP specification doesn't specify a direct way to do this. The RabbitMQ management plugin exposes a REST API that could be used to check the existence of a queue, which is a tempting approach, but not what AMQP offers by default, which is preferred. Moreover, this could expose the process to a check-then-act type of race condition.

Indeed, the queue could be created by another process after it is verified that it doesn't exist. Digging deep into the AMQP specification uncovers a feature that will handle this more elegantly, namely mandatory delivery. The `mandatory` field is part of the AMQP specification that tells RabbitMQ how to react if a message cannot be routed to a queue.

Consider the management REST API of RabbitMQ for cases when the AMQP specification doesn't have any way to support the functionality required. You can access the REST API documentation on the RabbitMQ broker at `http://localhost:15672/api/`.

When a message is published on an exchange with the `mandatory` flag set to `true`, it will be returned by RabbitMQ if the message cannot be delivered to a queue. A message cannot be delivered to a queue either because no queue is bound to the exchange or because none of the bound queues have a routing key that would match the routing rules of the exchange. In the current case, this would mean that no taxi inbox queue is bound to a routing key that matches the taxi ID.

The trick with returned messages is that RabbitMQ doesn't return them synchronously as a response to the publish operation: it returns them in an asynchronous fashion. This means that, for the developer, a specific message handler will have to be registered with RabbitMQ in order to receive the returned messages.

This leads to the overall architecture illustrated in the following diagram:

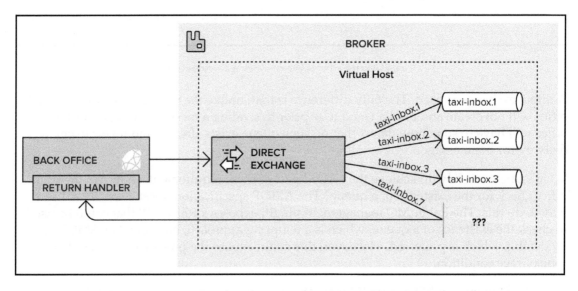

Fig 4.7: A dedicated handler takes care of returned messages

Messages published to a queue that does not exist are returned to the return handler. This handler is now in charge of making sure that the information message reaches the driver in some other way—for example, through email.

The default exchange type will be described before the new back office sender will be implemented.

Default exchanges in RabbitMQ

Each time a queue is created, it gets automatically bound to the default exchange with its queue name as the routing key. By publishing a message to the default exchange using the queue name as the routing key, the message will end up in the designated queue. This is also something that is going to be added into the following code example, in the *Implementing the back office sender* section.

What is this mysterious default exchange? It is a direct and durable exchange named " " (an empty string) that is automatically created by RabbitMQ for each virtual host.

To make the default exchange visible in the management console, its empty string name is rendered as the AMQP default, as shown in the following screenshot:

Fig 4.8: The default exchange is one among several built-in exchanges

As you can see, there are a host of other predeclared exchanges that are automatically created for every virtual host. They are easy to spot because their names start with **amq**. These exchanges are meant for testing and prototyping purposes only, so there is no need to use them in production.

Sending messages to the default exchange is a convenient way to reach a particular queue; however, do not overuse this pattern. It creates tight coupling between producers and consumers because the producer becomes aware of particular queue names.

With this explained, it's now time to add the necessary code to build this feature that was requested by the back office, which is implemented if a driver doesn't have an existing inbox queue.

Implementing the back office sender

CC's back office is now adding support for messages that were sent to drivers without a taxi inbox queue, messages that were returned. The Ruby client library, among other libraries, supports this feature very elegantly. The following is the required code to support the mandatory delivery of messages to taxi inboxes and to handle potentially returned messages.

Start out by requiring the bunny client library and then set up a connection and a channel to RabbitMQ, as described in Chapter 2, *Creating a Taxi Application*:

```
require "bunny"
 connection = Bunny.new ENV["RABBITMQ_URI"]

 connection.start
 channel = connection.create_channel
```

Then, declare a default exchange:

```
exchange = channel.default_exchange
```

A return handler is created, which handles the returned message:

```
exchange.on_return do |return_info, properties, content|
  puts "A returned message!"
end
```

Next, declare a durable inbox queue—in this example, named taxi-inbox.100:

```
queue = channel.queue("taxi-inbox.100", durable: true)
```

Subscribe to messages from RabbitMQ and give a simple notification to the developer. At this point, an email is sent, but please note that this example is kept short on purpose and doesn't include the method for actually sending the email:

```
queue.subscribe do |delivery_info, properties, content|
  puts "A message is consumed."
end
```

Messages are published with `routing_key` to target a particular taxi with the `mandatory` flag set to `true`. Since this queue is created and exists, this message should not be returned:

```
exchange.publish("A message published to a queue that does exist, it should
NOT be returned", :mandatory => true, :routing_key => queue.name)
```

Another mandatory message is published, but this time to a random queue. This message is going to be returned and handled by the return handler:

```
exchange.publish("A message published to a queue that does not exist, it
should be returned", :mandatory => true, :routing_key => "random-key")
```

Finally, close the connection:

```
connection.close
```

The preceding code example includes one message published to a queue that exists, while the other message is published to a queue with a random key name, a queue that does not exist. More code examples can be found at `http://rubybunny.info/articles/exchanges.html`.

That is all! The feature is ready to go live. Messages are returned asynchronously and there is no need to handle them the right way.

Summary

This chapter included information about message TTL and explored how to use message property name expiration values while looking at other important topics about tweaking message delivery. The information also described the use of dead-letter exchanges and queues. The chapter then took a look at how to use the default exchange and how to send mandatory messages.

CC is growing into a proper company and its platform is keeping right up with new features to meet the demands of drivers, customers, and back-office staff.

So far, only asynchronous interactions with RabbitMQ have been discussed, which makes sense because it's the core premise of messaging. That said, it's possible to perform synchronous operations too, as the next chapter demonstrates. The following chapter will include information on the direct interaction between the taxi and the client. What will the next feature rollout entail? The only way to find out is to keep reading!

5
Message Routing

Thus far, all message interaction in this book has been unidirectional, flowing from message publishers to consumers. What if a consumer wants to alert a publisher that processing is complete and send a reply, or a taxi driver wants to acknowledge a taxi booking request?

This chapter covers steps 5 to 10 in the taxi application system architecture, where a taxi driver responds to the customer and confirms a booking request. The taxi publishes its current location to a queue. The customer's application connects to the broker through WebSockets and subscribes to location updates, delivered directly from the taxi.

The **Remote Procedure Call** (**RPC**) request-response concept will be introduced, along with how to route a response back to the consumer. Since **Advanced Message Queuing Protocol** (**AMQP**) 0-9-1 , brokers provide four exchange types. This chapter also shows how to implement the last one, headers exchange.

Let's dive into the following topics:

- Sending responses to the publisher
- Reply-to queues and RPC
- Creating a data analysis service

Technical requirements

The code files of this chapter can be found on GitHub at `https://github.com/ PacktPublishing/RabbitMQ-Essentials-Second-Edition/tree/master/Chapter05`.

Sending responses to the publisher

It is true that all of our interactions with RabbitMQ so far have been one way and asynchronous. It is also true that clients interacting with a service usually expect to receive a response. Reversing the publisher and consumer roles in the response phase requires the client to act as a publisher and the service as a consumer.

Different queues are used for requests and responses, as demonstrated in `Chapter 2`, *Creating a Taxi Application*, and illustrated in the following diagram:

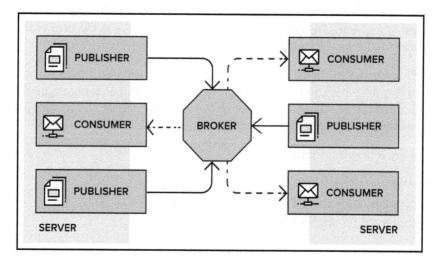

Fig 5.1: A request-response interaction performed with message queues

In the following diagram, *Fig 5.2*, we can see the following:

- When a taxi driver confirms a booking request, a message is sent to the message broker with information about the driver (**5**).
- The application service receives the message (**6**), stores the information in the database (**7**), and confirms the booking with the mobile application, which is ultimately shown to the customer (**8**).
- At this point, the taxi needs to continuously share its current location with the customer. This is accomplished by sending the car's latitude and longitude to a location queue every minute (**9**). The customer side of the app uses a WebSocket connection over RabbitMQ to subscribe to the current location queue (**10**).

Complete Car's (**CC**'s) architecture is shown in the following diagram, as a reminder:

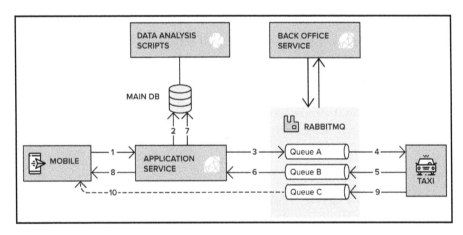

Fig 5.2: CC's main application architecture

Let's see how WebSockets is implemented.

WebSockets in RabbitMQ

RabbitMQ is a multi-protocol message broker. This section explores the **Single Text-Oriented Message Protocol** (**STOMP**) and how to use it with RabbitMQ to build interactive web applications. The Web STOMP RabbitMQ plugin makes it possible to use STOMP over the internet, by using WebSockets to send real-time data between a client—such as a web browser—and a broker via a web server. The plugin allows for highly interactive user experiences with data stored or processed on a server.

Start by enabling the Web STOMP plugin.

Enabling the Web STOMP plugin

As with the RabbitMQ management plugin, RabbitMQ does not embed the Web STOMP plugin by default but offers it as an option. The appropriate RabbitMQ plugin must be enabled as well as installed, and a **virtual host** (**vhost**) has to be created with the appropriate permissions.

Run the following Debian package script to install the Web STOMP plugin:

```
rabbitmq-plugins enable rabbitmq_web_stomp
```

For security purposes, create at least one user, with limited permissions, on a publicly exposed vhost. Run the following code to create the new vhost:

```
$ sudo rabbitmqctl add_vhost cc-dev-ws
Adding vhost "cc-dev-ws" ...
```

Next, add user permissions for the cc-dev user and the cc-dev-ws vhost:

```
$ sudo rabbitmqctl set_permissions -p cc-dev-ws cc-dev ".*" ".*" ".*"
Setting permissions for user "cc-dev" in vhost "cc-dev-ws" ..
```

The new vhost is now created and is accessible to the cc-dev user. Some basic security options should be configured before setting up a new queue for the taxis to publish their current locations.

Securing Web STOMP with SSL

Web STOMP uses the internet, which, in CC's application, leaves information vulnerable to snooping unless properly secured. Since most clients send the broker **Uniform Resource Locator** (**URL**), username, and password information, an additional level of security is necessary.

Luckily, it is possible to tell RabbitMQ to use **Secure Sockets Layer** (**SSL**) through the configuration file. For security, the CC team will add the following lines to the configuration to set up a certificate:

```
ssl_options.cacertfile = /path/to/tls/ca_certificate.pem

ssl_options.certfile = /path/to/tls/server_certificate.pem

ssl_options.keyfile = /path/to/tls/server_key.pem

ssl_options.verify = verify_peer

ssl_options.fail_if_no_peer_cert = true

stomp.default_user = guest

stomp.default_pass = guest

stomp.implicit_connect = true
```

For the settings to take effect, the broker must be restarted and the default username and password changed. The scripts contain the broker URL, which could give unwanted easy access to the server.

Creating and publishing GPS data to the queue

Now, the CC team will create a queue where the taxi sends the current location, this time by using `rabbitmqadmin` and running the following commands to create a queue called `taxi_information`:

```
rabbitmqadmin declare queue name=taxi_information durable=true vhost=cc-
dev-ws
```

Add an exchange called `taxi_exchange`, like this:

```
rabbitmqadmin declare exchange name=taxi_exchange type=direct vhost=cc-dev-
ws
```

Since the command-line tools do not allow the action to bind queues to exchanges, use the RabbitMQ management interface to bind the `taxi_information` queue to the `taxi_exchange` exchange using the `taxi_information` routing key.

The CC team will log in, head to the **Queues** section, and add this information to the **Bindings** section, as shown in the following diagram:

Fig 5.3: Add binding to the queue via RabbitMQ management

With a queue established, the taxi application can communicate with the broker. The code for this is not provided since it would be almost the same code as in Chapter 2, *Creating a Taxi Application*. Instead, the following diagram shows how a message can be published via the management console, which is usually used for testing purposes:

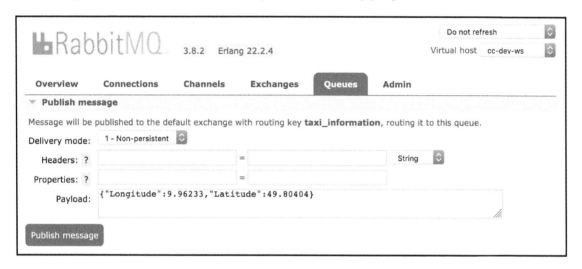

Fig 5.4: Send GPS coordinates to RabbitMQ

The consumer can now subscribe to **Global Positioning System** (**GPS**) data from the taxi_information queue.

Subscribing to GPS and driver information via WebSockets

The customer can use the mobile clients to receive location data through WebSockets, as shown in *Fig 5.2*.

The customer mobile application uses JavaScript and HTML, made possible with tools such as React Native or Angular NativeScript, which are two cross-platform frameworks that continue to gain traction.

The CC team imports the StompJs library (`stomp.umd.min.js`) into the application using a content delivery network, as follows:

```
<script
src="https://cdn.jsdelivr.net/npm/@stomp/stompjs@5.0.0/bundles/stomp.umd.min
.js"></script>
```

Then, CC includes some code, in order to receive updates from the queue.

First of all, the `stompClient` variable is declared and configured. The broker URL should start with `ws://` or `wss://`. The `reconnectDelay` variable in the example is set to 200 ms, which means that a retry will happen 200 ms after a disconnect, as follows:

```
let stompClient;

const stompConfig = {
  connectHeaders: {
   login: username,
    passcode: password,
    host: 'cc-dev-ws'
  },
  brokerURL: brokerURL,
  debug: function (str) {
    console.log('STOMP: ' + str);
  },
  reconnectDelay: 200,
  onConnect: function (frame) {
    const subscription =
stompClient.subscribe('/queue/taxi_information',
    function (message) {
      const body = JSON.parse(message.body);
      const latitude = body.latitude;
      const longitude = body.longitude;
    });
  }
};
```

After that, the instance is created and connected to, as follows:

```
stompClient = new StompJs.Client(stompConfig);
stompClient.activate();
```

The CC team will create a callback to handle incoming messages and subscribe directly to the `taxi_information` queue. The username, password, and broker URL must be changed.

The broker URL must include the Web STOMP port, defaulting to `15674`.

Happy times! The customer will now know approximately where the taxi is located, both before and during the ride.

Now, let's look at another option to receive a reply from the consumer.

Reply-to queues and RPC

The CC application can now communicate in a good way between the publisher and the consumer, but what if a function has to run on a remote computer and wait for the result? Hardcoding an exchange and routing key in the service to publish responses isn't possible as it would be too inflexible. The solution is to have the request message carry the coordinates of the location where the response should be sent, a pattern commonly known as RPC.

The application service calls a specific function residing on the taxi application, and the taxi sends the result to the end user. The request message carries the name of the queue where the response should be sent. The AMQP protocol supports this mechanism out of the box. The client can store the queue name of the location where the response must be sent.

When RabbitMQ delivers a message to the consumer, it will change the `reply-to` property. The server can reply to the message from the publisher by sending a message to the default exchange with the routing key of the `reply-to` property.

Any type of queue can be used for the `reply-to` mechanism, but in practice, the following two approaches are used:

- **Create a short-lived queue for each request-response interaction**. This approach uses an exclusive, auto-deleted, nondurable, server-side named queue created by the client with the following benefits:
    - No other consumer can get messages from it since it is exclusive.
    - It can be auto-deleted; once the reply has been consumed, there is no longer a use for it.
    - No need for it to be durable; request-response interactions are not meant to be long-lived.
    - The server generates a unique name, which relieves the client from having to figure out a unique naming scheme.

- **Use a permanent reply-to queue specific to the client**. This approach uses a nonexclusive, non-automatically deleted, nondurable, client-side named queue with the following benefits:
    - No need for it to be durable, for the same reason explained previously.
    - No need for it to be exclusive—a different consumer will be used for each request-response interaction.

The difficulty in using a permanent queue is in correlating responses with requests. This is done through the `CorrelationId` message property, carried from the request message to the response message. This property allows the client to identify the correct request to process.

A permanent queue is more efficient than using short-lived queues with each request since creation and deletion are expensive operations.

 RabbitMQ client libraries offer primitives that simplify responses correlated with requests.

That completes the information on routing back options to response queues through `reply-to`. To continue, the CC team will discover the fourth type of exchange offered by RabbitMQ by connecting a data analysis service.

Creating a data analysis service

CC wants to be able to analyze incoming data. This system analyses requests for taxis in different areas, discovers important patterns, and finds peak request times. The project manager assigned the team to build a system capable of running several versions of the same service in parallel, allowing the graceful evolution of the service during updates.

A member of the team stated that it is possible to use a topic exchange and structure the routing key as `{service_name}{version}`. Their idea works within the current system; however, RabbitMQ offers a more elegant solution to this problem through the headers exchange.

The headers exchange allows the routing of messages based on their headers, which are custom key-value pairs stored in the message properties. The custom key-value pairs guide messages to the correct queue or queues. With this approach, the message and its routing information are all self-contained, remain consistent, and are therefore easier to inspect as a whole.

This addition works flawlessly within CC's architecture, merely requiring the team to bind the queues to a headers exchange and send messages with the appropriate headers. Start by opening a command-line shell and executing the following commands:

1. Create a new headers exchange called `taxi_headers_exchange`, as follows:

   ```
   rabbitmqadmin declare exchange name=taxi_header_exchange
   type=headers --vhost cc-dev
   ```

   The CC team will set up a queue to receive information from the taxis.

2. Create a new queue called `taxi_information_with_headers`, as follows:

   ```
   rabbitmqadmin declare queue --name=taxi_information_with_headers
   durable=true --vhost cc-dev
   ```

Bind the new queue to the `taxi_header_exchange` headers exchange in the management console, as shown in the following screenshot:

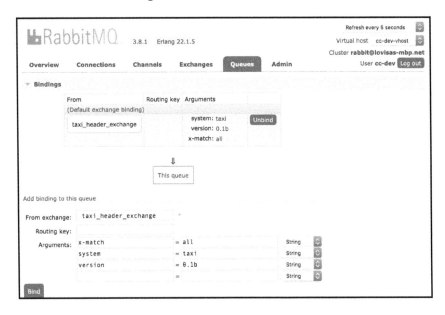

Fig 5.5: Bind a queue to an exchange in the management console

By setting **x-match** to **all**, this means that RabbitMQ will route messages sent to **taxi_header_exchange** to the **taxi_information_with_headers** queue only when **system = taxi** and **version = 0.1b**. Otherwise, the system drops the message. Header values to match on may be of the **String, Number, Boolean,** or **List** types. Routing keys aren't required since the key-value pairs serve as the key.

The **x-match** parameter specifies whether all headers must match or just one. The property can have two different values—**any** or **all**, described as follows:

- **all** is the default value, which means that all header pairs (key, value) must match.
- **any** means at least one of the header pairs must match.

Because the data analysis service is written in Python, we will switch away from Ruby for the moment. Luckily, connecting and publishing messages in Python is very much the same as it is in Ruby, so there is no big learning curve to get through.

Note that the RabbitMQ recommended library for Python is `pika` (`https://pypi. org/ project/pika/`). Information can be sent to the new queue as follows:

1. Start to import the client library `pika` and `json`:

    ```
    import pika
    import json
    ```

2. Set credentials to connect to RabbitMQ:

    ```
    credentials = pika.PlainCredentials("cc-dev", "taxi123")
    parameters = pika.ConnectionParameters(
      host="127.0.0.1",
      port=5672,
      virtual_host="cc-dev-ws",
      credentials=credentials)
    ```

3. Assert that the connection is established, and try to open a channel on the connection. Set the header version value to `0.1b` and the system value to `taxi`. A message is published to the `taxi_header_exchange` with the given GPS positions:

    ```
    conn = pika.BlockingConnection(parameters)
    assert conn.is_open
    try:
      ch = conn.channel()
      assert ch.is_open
      headers = {"version": "0.1b", "system": "taxi"}
    ```

```
    properties =
pika.BasicProperties(content_type='application/json',
headers=headers)
    message = {"latitude": 0.0, "longitude": -1.0}
    message = json.dumps(message)
    ch.basic_publish(
        exchange="taxi_header_exchange",
        body=message,
        properties=properties, routing_key="")
finally:
    conn.close()
```

Because `x-match=all`, both header values must be embedded in the message properties. The exchange ensures that the system and version match the values specified in the management console before routing the message to the `taxi_information_with_headers` queue.

Summary

As CC's users and customers become more familiar with the system, they begin to ask for more functionality. The CC application is now able to connect to the broker through WebSockets and subscribes to location updates delivered directly from the taxi. Location messages are flowing and CC's app is working great and offering more complex features.

This chapter further demonstrated how to use RPC in RabbitMQ via reply-to queues. The header exchange was introduced to build a system capable of running several versions of the same service in parallel, allowing graceful evolution during updates. Another exciting addition to the CC system took place in this chapter, which was the ability to incorporate data analysis into the system to discover important user patterns and other insights. Header exchanges were thereby explained.

The next chapter covers the all-important production realities that CC must understand going forward. Important topics such as federation features and clustering, along with health checks and alerts, are coming up.

Taking RabbitMQ to Production

6

At this point, **Complete Car** (**CC**) is running a single instance of RabbitMQ in production. Now CC also needs to ensure that the service is highly available. Creating clusters of nodes ensures that information is reachable even if systems go down. This chapter covers how to set up RabbitMQ clusters, including coverage of broker clustering, classic mirrored queues, and quorum queues. CC is also looking for a new elegant solution for log aggregation, where all logs are published to a centralized RabbitMQ node through the federation plugin, so this chapter will cover this topic as well.

To achieve CC's goal of nearly constant uptime, the topics in this chapter will include the following:

- Adding nodes to the cluster
- Discovering the types of RabbitMQ queues
- Using federated brokers and log aggregation

Technical requirements

The code files of this chapter can be found on GitHub at `https://github.com/PacktPublishing/RabbitMQ-Essentials-Second-Edition/tree/master/Chapter06`.

Adding nodes to the cluster

Things have been running smoothly for CC, but developers want to ensure that the system can survive a crash. A crash is always possible, even when using RabbitMQ. Power outages happen, sudden packet losses may corrupt updates, and administrators can improperly configure the system by accident. There is still a chance that, due to a glitch or error, an entire instance could be lost. Steps must be taken to address any issues that could lead to data loss, negative customer experience, or even the dreaded 2 a.m. phone call to the team.

The good news is that RabbitMQ provides the features needed to deal with potential crashes and other catastrophes right out of the box. RabbitMQ can be configured to run in an active-active deployment environment, meaning that two or more nodes actively run the same kind of service simultaneously. Several brokers can be engaged in a cluster to act as a single highly available **Advanced Message Queuing Protocol** (**AMQP**) service.

There is no need to resort to manual failover when using active-active deployment. No operation is needed if a broker goes down, sparing the team that 2 a.m. phone call. Depending on the number of active nodes in the high-availability cluster, a cluster can sustain several failures.

To avoid complications resulting from an unreachable broker, CC decides to start by rolling out a second RabbitMQ instance (named **rmq-prod-2**), clustering it with the one already used in production.

A RabbitMQ cluster is a logical grouping of one or several nodes, each sharing users, virtual hosts, queues, exchanges, and so on. The system architecture changes only inside the cluster, as seen in the following diagram:

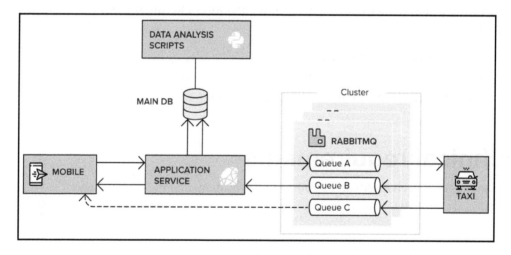

Fig 6.1: A high-availability cluster of many RabbitMQ brokers

More nodes are added into the RabbitMQ cluster. CC informs the team when the second instance of RabbitMQ is ready to be clustered with the existing one. To make this happen, the Erlang clustering feature will be used with RabbitMQ to allow local or remote communication between several Erlang nodes. Erlang clustering uses a security cookie as the mechanism for cross-node authentication. To avoid errors, the developers have made sure that the content of /var/lib/rabbitmq/.erlang.cookie is the same in each instance.

Note that a cluster will not work if a firewall blocks the RabbitMQ instances from communicating with each other. If that happens, open the specific ports used by AMQP (defaulting to `5672`) so that the cluster will work. Get more information at, `http://www.rabbitmq.com/clustering.html#firewall`.

There is no need to configure any users or virtual hosts on the second node as done in `Chapter 1`, *A Rabbit Springs to Life*. Just join the cluster and the configuration will automatically synchronize with the existing RabbitMQ instance, including users, virtual hosts, exchanges, queues, and policies.

Keep in mind that a node completely resets when it joins a cluster. RabbitMQ deletes all configuration and data before synchronizing with the other nodes.

To join a node to a cluster, first stop RabbitMQ, then join the cluster, and finally restart the RabbitMQ application:

```
$ sudo rabbitmqctl stop_app
# => Stopping node rabbit@rmq-prod-2 ...
# => ...done.
$ sudo rabbitmqctl join_cluster rabbit@rmq-prod-1
# => Clustering node rabbit@rmq-prod-2 with rabbit@rmq-prod-1 ...
# => ...done.
$ sudo rabbitmqctl start_app
# => Starting node rabbit@rmq-prod-2 ...
# => ...done.
```

Make sure the same major version of Erlang is used by all the RabbitMQ nodes or the `join_cluster` command might fail. It is possible to run a cluster with mixed Erlang versions, but there can be incompatibilities that will affect cluster stability.

RabbitMQ also requires the use of the same major/minor version across nodes up to and including 3.7.x. It is possible to run different patch versions (for example, 3.7.X and 3.7.Y) most of the time, except when indicated otherwise in the release notes.

Feature flags is a mechanism new to RabbitMQ version 3.8. These flags define a RabbitMQ node's ability to become a part of a cluster. Feature flags control which features are considered enabled or available on all cluster nodes, so nodes using the subsystem must have the same dependencies. Read more at `https://www.rabbitmq.com/feature-flags.html`.

After running the preceding commands, check to see whether the cluster is active by running the `cluster_status` command on any node:

```
$ sudo rabbitmqctl cluster_status
# => Cluster status of node rabbit@rmq-prod-1 # ->
# => [{nodes,[{disc,[rabbit@rmq-prod-2,rabbit@rmq-prod-1]}]},
{running_nodes,[rabbit@rmq-prod-2,rabbit@rmq-prod-1]}, {partitions,[]}]
# => ...done.
```

Notice how two lists of nodes are given in the status message. In this case, the nodes are the list of configured nodes in the cluster. The list named `running_nodes` contains those that are actually active. Configured nodes are persistent, meaning they will survive broker restarts since each broker automatically re-engages with the cluster.

Confirm that the new node will synchronize with the cluster by connecting to the management console on another node (**rmq-prod-2**). Use the **cc-admin** user to log in and go to the **Queues** view.

The configuration should be synchronized as shown in the following screenshot:

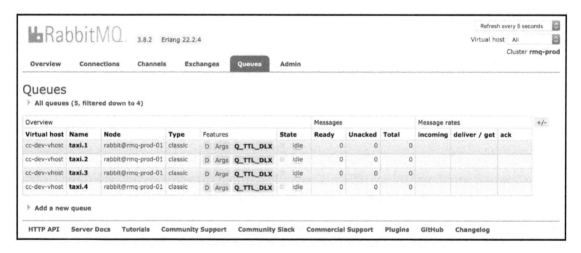

Fig 6.2: All configurations are synchronized after joining the cluster

To add more nodes, let each new node join another node in the cluster. The **Overview** tab in the management console of the first node shows all the nodes that are in the cluster, which are automatically discovered, as shown in the following screenshot:

Fig 6.3: The management console overview shows all cluster members

As shown, all members of the cluster are listed along with basic statistics and ports. The different values shown in the **Info** column are as follows:

- **basic**: Describes the `rates_mode`, which tells how the queues report statistics. This can be one of `basic` (the default), `detailed`, or `none`.
- **disc**: Means that the node persists data to the filesystem, which is the default behavior. It is also possible to start a node in **RAM** mode, where all message data is stored in memory, which can speed up systems provided that they have enough memory.
- **7**: Shows the number of plugins that are enabled.
- **allocated**: Describes the memory calculation strategy.

Nodes can be removed (`http://www.rabbitmq.com/clustering.html#breakup`) from the cluster through `rabbitmqctl`, the command-line tool for managing a RabbitMQ server node.

All CC applications are currently connecting to one single RabbitMQ node. This needs to be modified. Applications should try to connect to one node first and fail over to another node if the original attempt fails. Read on to see how that is done.

Connecting to the cluster

All CC applications currently connect to a single RabbitMQ node, which needs to be modified to benefit from the advantages of the cluster. All applications connecting to RabbitMQ need to be modified. The applications should try to connect to one node first, failing over to another if the original attempt fails. This is the only required change; the applications will interact with the broker as they did before.

First, modify the main application connection Ruby code as follows:

```
begin
  connection = Bunny.new(
    hosts: ['rmq-prod-01', 'rmq-prod-02'])
  connection.start
  rescue Bunny::TCPConnectionFailed => e
    puts "Connection to server failed"
end
```

Basically, the list of broker addresses is passed. With this in place, the RabbitMQ Ruby client will connect to the first responsive node in the address list and will try each of the provided broker addresses until it can establish a connection or eventually fails. In the case of failure, the overall reconnect mechanism that's already in place will kick in and the addresses will once again be attempted for connection.

> It is possible to manually synchronize a mirrored queue using the `rabbitmqctl sync_queue <queue_name>` command. Cancel the synchronization with `rabbitmqctl cancel_sync_queue <queue_name>`.

At this point, there is only one more step to perform to ensure the high availability of the queue data: enabling a way to spread the data to the other node(s). The options available are **classic mirrored queues** and **quorum queues**. But first, some partition handling strategies.

Partition handling strategies

Adding even more nodes to the cluster is of course possible. However, this brings a new challenge in the form of network connectivity. Split-brains and early message confirmation are common issues when using more than one node. Split-brains occur in distributed systems when a portion of the network becomes unreachable from another portion, creating network partitions (called a **netsplit**). To avoid this situation, set a partition handling strategy. In RabbitMQ, this is set through the `cluster_partition_handling` parameter in the configuration file – `https://www.rabbitmq.com/partitions.html#automatic-handling`.

The **pause-minority** strategy terminates nodes in the minority partition. This is the default way to resolve split-brains in many distributed networks. The **pause-if-all-down** feature only pauses a node if none are reachable. This is inadvisable as it creates large discrepancies between the data in each partition.

Once nodes become available in the **pause-if-all-down** setting, two more options are available to specify how to reconnect the network. Simply ignore another partition or auto-heal the cluster. The nodes the system cannot pause must also be specified. In the **pause-minority** strategy, the partitions reconnect when available.

RabbitMQ ensures synchronization across clusters. Clients can reach their exchanges and queues over any node; however, the messages themselves are not carried over. The next section covers how that can be done.

Discovering the types of RabbitMQ queues

Queues in RabbitMQ can be durable or transient. Classic mirrored queues are recommended for transient message handling, while quorum queues are a good alternative for durable queues.

Durable queue metadata is stored on disk while a transient queue stores it in memory, when possible. Another queue type, lazy queues, writes the contents to disk as early as possible for both durable and transient messages.

Due to technical limitations in classic mirrored queues, it is difficult to make guarantees on how failures are handled. The RabbitMQ documentation (`https://www.rabbitmq.com/ha.html`) recommends that users get familiar with quorum queues and consider them instead of classic mirrored queues where possible.

Mirroring queues

In the case of CC, the data in the queues needs to be highly available. Mirrored queues provide this type of security. Queue mirroring uses a master-mirror design pattern. All message queuing and dequeuing actions happen with the master, and the mirrors receive the updates periodically from the master. If a master becomes unavailable, RabbitMQ promotes a mirror to a master; usually, the oldest mirror becomes the new master, as long as it is synchronized.

> It is also possible to set up a master-master system by sending data to a different cluster in addition to the original. This provides a useful backup for hardware updates and extreme cases of failure. It can also help speed up interaction in different geographic regions.

Telling the cluster how to mirror queues must in our case be done via the Q_TTL_DLX policy since only one policy at a time is allowed in a queue or exchange. The first step is to clear the policy created in Chapter 4, *Tweaking Message Delivery*, then applying a new policy combining the Q_TTL_DLX policy with one created for queue mirroring.

Run the following commands to change the Q_TTL_DLX policy and tell RabbitMQ how to mirror queues. Start by clearing the policy:

```
$ sudo rabbitmqctl clear_policy -p cc-prod-vhost Q_TTL_DLX
# => Clearing policy "Q_TTL_DLX"
# => ......done.
"Specify the new HA_Q_TTL_DLX policy:"
$ sudo rabbitmqctl set_policy -p cc-prod-vhost HA_Q_TTL_DLX "taxi\.\d+"
'{"message-ttl":604800000, "dead-letter-exchange":"taxi-dlx", "ha-
mode":"all", "ha-sync-mode":"automatic"}' --apply-to queues
# => Setting policy "HA_Q_TTL_DLX" for pattern "taxi\.\d+" to "{\"ha-
mode\":\"all\", \"message-ttl\":604800000, \"dead-letter-exchange\":\"taxi-
dlx\"}" with priority "0"
# => ......done.
```

Alternatively, add the policy from the management console, as shown in the following screenshot:

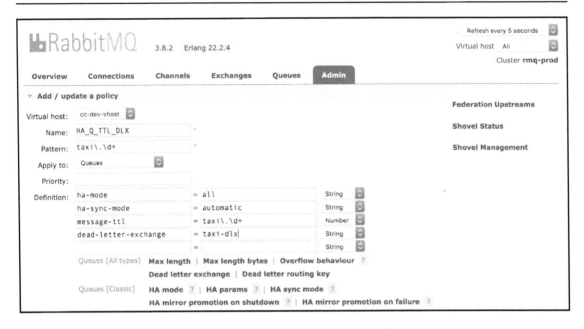

Fig 6.4: Policy added via the RabbitMQ management console

High availability mode has been added to the existing **TTL** and **DLX** policy rules. The **all** value for **ha-mode** tells RabbitMQ to mirror queues across all nodes in the cluster, which is exactly what CC wants in their two-node cluster. The other options are **exactly** and **nodes**, allowing developers to specify the number of nodes when using the exact option and a list of node names when using the **nodes** option through the **ha-params** parameters.

The **ha-sync-mode** parameter is used to specify the synchronization mode for the mirrored queue. This parameter can be set to **manual** or **automatic**. In manual mode, a newly mirrored queue will not receive any existing messages but will eventually become consistent with the master queue as consumers retrieve messages. This reduces overhead at the cost of losing information. Automatic mode sends messages to each queue, meaning a small hit to the system performance.

CC decides to use immediate queue synchronization so that any existing messages become visible across all nodes nearly instantaneously. CC is fine with the initial unresponsiveness this creates since performance is not critical for user messages.

Navigate to the **Queues** tab in the management console after running the preceding command. Observe that the **HA_Q_TTL_DLX** policy has been applied to the intended queues:

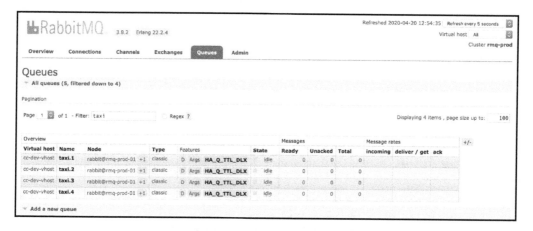

Fig 6.5: Mirrored queues with the high availability policies applied

Notice how the mirrored queues have a **+1** next to them. This denotes the fact that the queues are mirrored to another node in the cluster. The master (**rabbit@rmq-prod-1**) and the mirror nodes (**rabbit@rmq-prod-2**) are clearly defined in the **Details** section of each queue in the management console as well, as seen in the following screenshot:

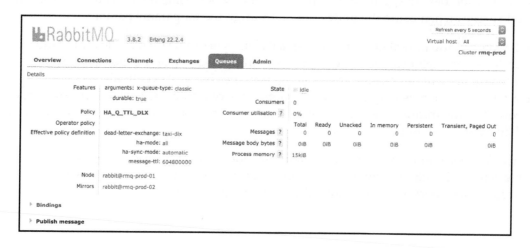

Fig 6.6: Master and mirror nodes are detailed

At this point, the RabbitMQ brokers are clustered and taxi order request queues are mirrored. Client applications can benefit from this highly available deployment and connect to different nodes.

 Setting the Master Queue Location: Every queue has a primary replica known as the queue master. This queue is the first to receive messages before synchronization. It is possible to influence how this is set using the **x-queue-master-locator** parameter in the **Queues** tab of the management console or when creating a queue programmatically.

Quorum queues are a new type of queue, often recommended over classic mirrored queues.

Quorum queues

As an alternative to durable mirrored queues, quorum queues ensure that the cluster is up to date by agreeing on the contents of a queue. In doing so, quorum queues avoid losing data, which could occur with mirrored queues when messages are confirmed too early. Quorum queues are available as of RabbitMQ 3.8.0. As detailed in the RabbitMQ documentation (`https://www.rabbitmq.com/quorum-queues.html`), some transient features are not available when using quorum queues.

A quorum queue has a leader that roughly serves the same purpose as it did for the classic mirrored queue master. All communication is routed to the queue leader, which means the queue leader locality has an effect on the latency and bandwidth requirement of the messages; however, the effect should be lower than it was in classic mirrored queues.

In quorum queues, the leader and replication are consensus-driven, which means they agree on the state of the queue and its contents. While mirrored queues may confirm messages too early and lose data, quorum queues will only confirm when the majority of its nodes are available, which thereby avoids data loss.

Declare a quorum queue using the following command:

```
rabbitmqadmin declare queue name=<name> durable=true arguments='{"x-queue-
type": "quorum"}'
```

These queues must be durable and instantiated by setting the `x-queue-type` header to `quorum`. If the majority of nodes agree on the contents of a queue, the data is valid. Otherwise, the system attempts to bring all queues up to date.

Quorum queues have support for the handling of poison messages, which are messages that are never consumed completely or positively acknowledged.

The number of unsuccessful delivery attempts can be tracked and displayed in the x-delivery-count header. A poison message can be dead-lettered when it has been returned more times than configured.

Lazy queues are another queue type worth exploring, so read on.

Lazy queues

Queues can become long for various reasons including consumer maintenance or the arrival of large batches of messages. While RabbitMQ can support millions of messages, keeping queues as short as possible is recommended by most experts. Messages are stored in memory by default. RabbitMQ then flushes messages (page out) to free up the RAM usage when the queue becomes too long for the underlying instance to handle. Storing messages in RAM enables faster delivery of messages to consumers than storing them to disk.

The page out function usually takes time and often stops the queue from processing messages, which deteriorates the queue speed. For this reason, queues that contain a lot of messages can have a negative impact on the broker's performance. Additionally, it takes a lot of time to rebuild the index after a cluster is restarted and to sync messages between nodes.

Beginning with RabbitMQ version 3.6, a policy called lazy queues was added to enable the storage of messages to disk automatically in order to minimize RAM usage. Lazy queues can be enabled by setting the mode via the queue.declare arguments or by applying a policy to all queues.

 Persistent messages can be written to the disk as they enter the broker and be kept in RAM at the same time.

Different queue types have been shown, and it's time to look into how CC should handle log aggregation from all clusters.

Using federated brokers and log aggregation

The way a cluster of two RabbitMQ brokers is created is really similar to what is typically done when making a relational database highly available. The database remains a centralized resource offering high guarantees of availability. Still, RabbitMQ is not a one-trick rabbit when it comes to high availability.

To form a picture of a RabbitMQ system, the following two plugins allow broker connection:

- **Shovel**: Connects queues and exchanges between different brokers
- **Federation**: Forms cross-broker connections for queues to queues, or exchanges to exchanges

Both plugins ensure the reliable delivery of messages across brokers by routing them as instructed or offering a safe place for them to remain until they can be dealt with. Neither requires the brokers to be clustered, which simplifies setup and management. Moreover, both plugins work fine over WAN connections, which isn't the case in a clustering scenario.

Configure the destination node in a federation manually. The upstream nodes are configured automatically. On the other hand, shovels must have each source node configured manually to send to a destination node, which itself doesn't require any configuration.

The CC team is requesting a good way to process logs, and they quickly realize that the federation plugin suits the process well.

Handling log processing

CC's system is growing and growing, and so is the team of taxi drivers and developers. The team that is in charge of analytics has been looking for an elegant solution to aggregate logs from different applications in order to roll out new statistics, both for internal and end-user consumption. Fortunately, RabbitMQ can be used for application log processing thanks to its high performance.

In this topology, all applications will write to a local RabbitMQ node, which will act as a store-and-forward broker, pushing all logs to a centralized RabbitMQ node as shown in the following diagram:

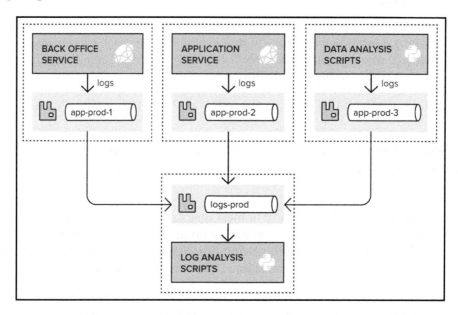

Fig 6.7: A topology that federates log messages to a central broker

If this central node is down, the log entries will remain locally accumulated until it comes back up. Messages flow through an exchange in one location (called the **upstream**) to be replicated to exchanges in other locations (the **downstream**), as seen in the following diagram:

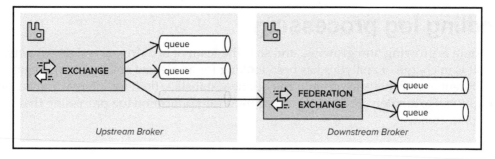

Fig 6.8: Exchange federation message flow

Obviously, the assumption here is that the local RabbitMQ nodes are extremely stable. The experience with running RabbitMQ in the past few months will help with this approach. Moreover, logs are considered important but not critical data for CC, so a best-effort approach is acceptable. Knowing this, the team chooses to use the federation plugin, as it's the one that supports federation to queue connectivity (with the shovel plugin, messages would have to be accumulated in a local queue on each node).

Remember, all queues that were mirrored in the previous section were queues that matched the `taxi-inbox\.\d+` regex pattern. All log queues mentioned now are left out of the equation. That's how the CC team wants it, as they don't want to mirror such highly trafficked queues. What could be done in order for CC to enjoy the same guarantees for log aggregation? Enter the notion of messaging topologies.

 More information on the shovel plugin can be found at `http://www.rabbitmq.com/shovel.html`.

The federation plugin needs to be installed on all RabbitMQ nodes that will engage in the topology by running the following commands on each node:

```
$ sudo rabbitmq-plugins enable rabbitmq_federation
Applying plugin configuration to rabbit@app-prod-1...

$ sudo rabbitmq-plugins enable rabbitmq_federation_management
Applying plugin configuration to rabbit@app-prod-1...
```

Moreover, unlike with clustering, each node needs to be manually set up to have the desired user and virtual host configured. As discussed in Chapter 1, *A Rabbit Springs to Life*, it is time to run the necessary command. Next, the `apps-log` exchange federation itself must be configured. This involves multiple steps (detailed shortly) that are all run on the central broker, the one toward which all logs will converge, the downstream.

First, the upstreams are configured, which are the RabbitMQ nodes that will send data to the central broker. Three upstreams are needed since there are three servers that will send logs, `app-prod-1`, `app-prod-2`, and `app-prod-3`; however, in the interest of brevity, only two nodes will be shown in the following example.

An upstream can be added via `rabbitmqctl`:

```
# Adds a federation upstream named "app-prod-logs"
rabbitmqctl -p logs-prod set_parameter federation-upstream app-prod-logs
'{"uri":"amqp://cc-prod:******@app-prod-1:5672/cc-prod-vhost"}'
```

Alternatively, the policy can be added via the management console:

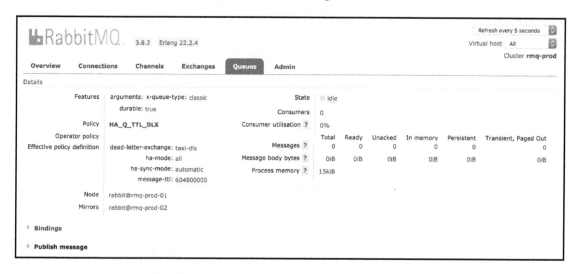

Fig 6.9: Add a federation upstream named app-prod-logs to the downstream broker

Once an upstream has been specified in the downstream, a policy that controls the federation can be added to the downstream server as well. The **app-prod-logs** federation is added just like any other policy (`https://www.rabbitmq.com/parameters.html#policies`) by using the terminal:

```
rabbitmqctl set_policy -p logs-prod --apply-to exchanges log-exchange-
federation "^app-logs*" '{"federation-upstream-set":"all"}' --apply-to
exchanges
```

The policy can also be added through the management console:

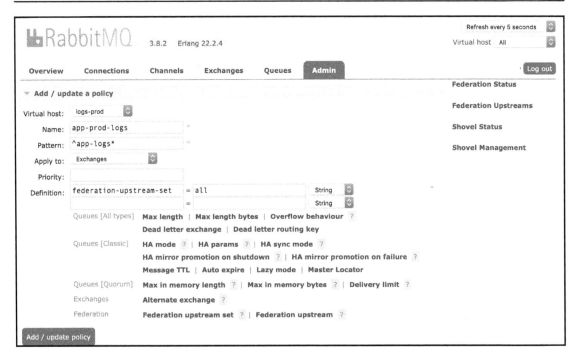

Fig 6.10: Federation policy added to the downstream server

The CC team does this by applying a policy that matches the exchange names. The pattern argument is a regular expression used to match queue (or exchange) names. In CC's case, the federation policy is applied to all exchanges with names beginning with `app-prod`.

A policy can apply to an upstream set or to a single exchange or queue upstream. In this example, `federation-upstream-set` is applied to all upstreams.

 If it is certain that there will never be more than one logical group of upstreams, the creation of an upstream set is skipped in favor of using the implicit set named `all`, which automatically contains all the upstreams in a virtual host.

In this case, it is good to make sure that the user that the federation plugin will use in the central broker to interact with the federated exchange is also configured.

Browse to the **Federation Upstreams** tab in the **Admin** section of the management console, which will show that the upstream has been correctly configured, as shown in the following screenshot:

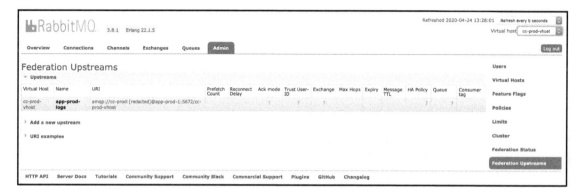

Fig 6.11: Upstream nodes are configured in a federation

Switching to **Federation Status** shows an empty screen as it's inactive. Why is that? After all, the topology was just created. The reason is that no exchange or queue is actively engaged in the topology yet. Because of its dynamic nature, the federation is inactive. Creating the **app-logs** exchange on both the upstream and the downstream servers and binding the **app-logs** exchange to queues is the next step before returning to the **Federation Status** tab. It is here noted that the federation is now running links for the **app-logs** exchange from the two upstream nodes of the configured set. See the following screenshot:

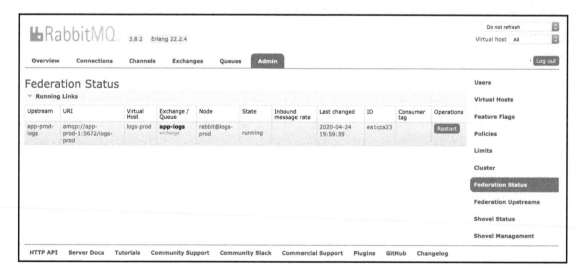

Fig 6.12: Running upstream links for a federated exchange

It's possible to get the status of the federation from the command line by running `sudo rabbitmqctl eval rabbit_federation_status:status()` on the downstream node.

The **Connections** and **Channels** tabs of the management console now show that the downstream node is connected to the upstream node over the AMQP protocol, as seen in the following screenshot:

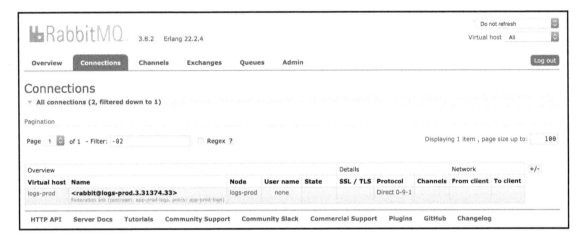

Fig 6.13: Federation link in the Connections tab

Except for the setup of the topology itself, there's nothing magical about the federation. It's been built on top of AMQP, and thus benefits from the same advantages offered by the protocol. Hence, if the RabbitMQ instances are firewalled, no special port other than the one used by AMQP (`5672` by default) needs to be opened.

Read more about the federation plugin at `http://www.rabbitmq.com/federation.html` and `http://www.rabbitmq.com/federation-reference.html`.

Summary

The CC example has provided information on how to create a basic message queue architecture, add valuable features to meet user demand, and keep a system running flawlessly. This chapter covered how RabbitMQ delivers powerful features through clustering and federation and how these features increase the availability and overall resilience of the messaging infrastructure. Quorum, classic mirrored, and lazy queues were also explored.

Along the way, information and guidance on best practices for a reliable, resilient system were offered. The next chapter highlights these recommendations and provides key takeaways from CC's journey through RabbitMQ. It also explores monitoring of RabbitMQ.

Best Practices and Broker Monitoring

7

The previous chapters of this book focused on the setup of a successful microservice architecture using RabbitMQ at the example company **Complete Car** (**CC**). Many RabbitMQ features were included, however, no system is complete without an understanding of the best practices to use in its implementation. As with all production systems, proper monitoring and alerts are also needed to stay on top of things.

CC's cluster is stable and there are no performance issues. This chapter summarizes the key takeaways learned from CC's system, including best practices and recommendations for queues, routing, exchanges, message handling, and more.

This chapter explores the following topics:

- How to avoid losing messages
- Keeping queues and brokers clean
- Routing best practices
- Networking over connections and channels
- Exploring key takeaways
- Monitoring – querying the REST API

This chapter is an ideal reference guide when setting up infrastructure using RabbitMQ. Refer back to the key takeaways, best practices, and monitoring tips in this chapter for valuable insights when putting RabbitMQ into production.

How to avoid losing messages

Losing messages can be avoided by following the best practices in this section. For the most part, CC has followed the best practice of **keeping queues short** and efficient. Queues that contain too many messages have a negative impact on the broker's performance. An identified **high RAM usage** could indicate that the number of queued messages rapidly went up.

Here are some best practice recommendations for how to not lose messages in RabbitMQ:

- Use at least three nodes in the RabbitMQ cluster, and the **quorum queue** type to spread messages to different nodes.
- If it is absolutely imperative that all messages are processed, declare a queue as **durable** and set the message delivery mode to **persistent**, as described in Chapter 2, *Creating a Taxi Application*. Queues, exchanges, and messages need to be able to handle any restarts, crashes, or hardware failures that may occur.

Here are some clarifications regarding message handling in RabbitMQ:

- Understanding the trade-offs that come with persistence is essential when designing a durable system architecture. **Lazy queues**, though using transient messages, have a similar effect on performance.
- Using transient messages with durable queues creates speed without losing configuration but may result in message loss.

What if all these best practices are followed and messages are still in jeopardy of being lost? The next section covers the dead letter exchange, so messages that would potentially be gone forever have a place to wait until they can be processed.

Using a dead letter exchange

Even when using durable queues and persistent messages, issues can occur that result in unhandled messages. A TTL might be set, a queue length might have been exceeded or the message might have been negatively acknowledged by the consumer. As a best practice, the routing key of the message should specify x-dead-letter-routing-key so that the message is never dropped. Attach queues to the exchange and manage messages programmatically. Try to avoid sending messages to the same exchange as this may result in a form of infinite recursion. Some messages might be unmanageable to handle and continually end up in the exchange. Make sure to handle these errors in the programming logic.

Set the `x-dead-letter-routing-key` property in the declaration of a queue. This helps with performance and separate error handling by components in the architecture, as described in `Chapter 4`, *Tweaking Message Delivery*.

It is recommended for applications that often get hit by spikes of messages to set a queue max-length. The queue max-length helps keeping the queue short by discarding messages from the head of the queue. The max-length can be set to a number of messages, or a set number of bytes.

Handling acknowledgments and confirms

In the event of a connection failure, a message in transit may get lost. Acknowledgments provide an alert to the server and the clients if messages need to be retransmitted. The client can either ack the message when it is received or when it has processed the message. However, it is important to remember that the application that consumes important messages should not ack until handled. That way, unprocessed messages from crashes or exceptions don't end up being missed. A publisher confirmation requires the server to confirm a message has been received from a publisher.

Confirms can also have an impact on system performance, but they are required if the publisher must process messages at least once.

Best practices of message handling

Queues and clients handle the burden of their payloads – messages. To further improve performance, fine-tune messages and message handling.

Limiting message size

The number of messages sent per second is a much larger concern than the size of the messages themselves. However, sending large messages is not a best practice, and neither is sending too small messages since AMQP adds a small packet overhead to all messages sent.

Examine messages to see whether they can be split and sent to different queues, as follows:

- Split iterable data into chunks and send a small chunk per message.
- Store large files in a distributed store, such as Hadoop or networked attached storage.

- Split the architecture into more modular components with a queue per component.
- Offload appropriate metadata to a key-value store.

While sending large messages can be avoided, bandwidth, architecture, and fail-over limits are a consideration. The size of the message will depend on the application but should be as small as possible.

Using consumers and prefetching

Setting a prefetch value distributes workloads evenly across the system. Prefetching is allowed in RabbitMQ, but it is important to remember that prefetching is only effective when all consumers are busy.

RabbitMQ must manage consumption across queues and consumers. A prefetch value that is too low keeps the consumers idle as they wait for messages to arrive, which in turn will slow down the broker's ability to handle requests. Setting the prefetch value too high keeps one consumer busy while the rest remain idle, as described in `Chapter 3`, *Sending Messages to Multiple Taxi Drivers*.

If processing time is low and the network is stable, then the prefetch value can be increased. In this case, the prefetch value can be determined easily by dividing the total round trip time by the processing time.

If there are many consumers and a longer processing time, the prefetch value trends lower. If processing times are long enough, set the prefetch limit to 1.

As queues get busier with demand, more system resources are consumed. Keeping the queues and brokers clean is imperative for good performance, which is covered in the next section.

Keeping queues and brokers clean

A clean broker is an efficient broker. To keep power and space at an optimum level, making sure queues and brokers are clean is easy. RabbitMQ provides mechanisms for auto-deleting messages and queues to keep space free. These include setting the **time to live** (**TTL**) and auto-deletion of unused queues, which are detailed in the following sections.

Setting the TTL for messages or the max-length on queues

Queues providing messaging support for long-running processes may grow extremely large. A too large queue might affect the performance of the broker. Setting the **TTL** allows messages to be removed from the queue after a certain time. If specified, these messages enter the dead letter exchange. This saves more messages and even handles potential issues without losing data.

Set a reasonable **TTL** with the `x-message-ttl` property when declaring a queue. Make sure to provide `x-dead-letter-exchange` and `x-dead-letter-routing-key` to avoid losing messages entirely.

It is recommended for applications that often get hit by spikes of messages to set a queue max-length. The queue max-length helps keeping the queue short by discarding messages from the head of the queue. The max-length can be set to a number of messages, or a set number of bytes.

Auto-deleting unused queues

In addition to keeping queues from becoming overly large, queues can be dropped based on use.

There are three ways to delete an unused queue automatically, as follows:

1. Set an expiration policy for the queue using the `x-expires` property on the declaration, keeping queues alive only for a number of non-zero milliseconds when unused.
2. Set the `auto-delete` queue property to `true` on the declaration. This means the queue will be dropped after the following scenarios:

   - The initial connection is made.
   - The last consumer shuts down.
   - The channel/connection is closed or the queue has lost the **Transmission Control Protocol** (**TCP**) connection with the server.

3. Set the exclusive property to `true` on queue declaration so that the structure belongs to the declaring connection and is deleted when the connection closes.

Sometimes, the journey itself is what creates inefficiency in a message queue. To make sure messages are taking the best path possible, follow the best practices for routing found in the next section.

Routing best practices

As a best practice, direct exchanges are the fastest to use. Even when using direct exchanges, those with multiple bindings require more time to calculate where messages must be sent. There are some additional best practices to consider for routing.

Designing a system with routing in mind

Every endpoint is a service or application. Unlike CC, which operates between a car and, for the most part, a single application layer, many microservice architectures pass messages through dozens of services.

CC designed their system architecture around small services. They combined operations where it did make sense. After designing a smaller system, they consider where additional exchanges or queues could be beneficial. This kept the overall design small enough without limiting processing power.

Networking over connections and channels

Thousands of connections add up to a heavy burden on a RabbitMQ server, causing it to run out of memory and crash. A large number of connections and channels can also negatively impact the RabbitMQ management interface due to the large number of performance metrics being processed. To avoid this, configure each application to create an extremely small number of connections – 1, if possible. Instead of using multiple connections, establish a channel for each thread. Each connection should be long-lived and the following best practices should be considered depending on the application structure.

Remember that even if new hardware offers hundreds of threads, only the number of channels set can be established and this number should be kept from growing too large. As some clients don't make channels thread-safe, it is best not to share channels between threads. Doing so may create a race condition, which could completely crash the application.

Repeatedly opening and closing connections and channels is also detrimental to system performance. Doing so increases latency as more TCP packets are sent over the network.

Using TLS and AMQPS for security

RabbitMQ can be connected over AMQPS, which is the AMQP protocol wrapped in TLS. Data passed over the network is encrypted, but there is a performance impact to consider. To maximize performance, use VPC or VPN peering instead since they provide a private, isolated environment for traffic and do not involve the AMQP client and server directly.

Do not expose the backend over the frontend. The CC example is simplified. In reality, there would likely be an application layer added between unknown users and the broker.

Separate connections

By default, RabbitMQ will reduce the speed of connections that publish too quickly for queues to keep up. RabbitMQ simply applies back-pressure on the TCP connection, which places it in flow control. A flow-controlled connection shows a state of flow in the management UI and through HTTP API responses. This means the connection is experiencing blocking and unblocking several times a second to keep the message flow rate at a level that the rest of the server and the queues can handle.

When the publisher is using the same TCP connection as the consumer, messages can be blocked while replying to the broker. The server may not receive the acks from the client, which will have a negative impact on the speed and cause it to be overwhelmed. Achieving higher throughput is, therefore, best accomplished through separate connections for publishers and consumers.

Splitting queues over different cores

The CC infrastructure runs on multiple cores. To achieve better performance, queues are split among different cores and nodes. Queues in RabbitMQ are bound to the node where they are first declared. This holds true even for clustered brokers, as all messages routed to a specific queue go to the node where the queue lives. One queue in RabbitMQ can handle up to 50,000 messages a second. Better performance is therefore achieved when queues are split over different cores and nodes, and when they are spread between multiple queues.

It is possible to manually split queues evenly between nodes, but this can be difficult to remember. Alternatively, there are two plugins to assist with organizing multiple nodes or a single node cluster with multiple cores. These are the **Consistent Hash Exchange** and the **RabbitMQ sharding** plugins.

RabbitMQ sharding

Sharding makes it easy to distribute messages among queues on different nodes. A queue can be spread among multiple actual queues. Once an exchange is defined as sharded, the supporting queues automatically start on every cluster node with messages spreading accordingly, as shown in the following diagram:

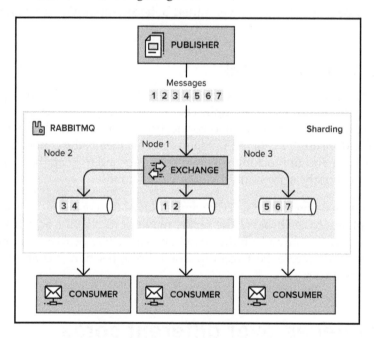

Fig 7.1: Sharding among queues

The routing keys ensure an even distribution of messages among queues. The plugin expects you to run a consumer per shard with new nodes being automatically incorporated. Note that it's important to consume from all queues. The plugin provides a centralized place to send messages, and load-balances messages across nodes by adding queues across the cluster. Read more about the RabbitMQ sharding plugin at: `https://github.com/rabbitmq/rabbitmq-sharding`.

Consistent Hash Exchange

RabbitMQ offers another plugin that helps load-balance messages through the Consistent Hash Exchange. Based on the routing key, **bound** queues in this exchange are sent messages equally. This optimizes the use of a cluster with multiple cores, as the plugin creates a hash of the routing key and is consistent about spreading messages between queues bound to the exchange, ensuring optimal use over many cores in a cluster.

Read more about the Consistent Hash Exchange plugin at: `https://github.com/rabbitmq/rabbitmq-consistent-hash-exchange`.

Exploring key takeaways

For the sake of simplification, optimization can be broken into two forms, and since cars have been a popular topic in this book, let's stick with that theme.

Ferrari – fast and smooth: If the system must have fast performance and high throughput, use a single node. Keep queues as short as possible, and set the max length or TTL if possible. Do not set the lazy queue policies to keep retrieval time short. Use transient messages, rather than persistent ones, for the same reason. Take advantage of using multiple queues and consumers, providing maximum throughput. For the fastest possible throughput, manual acks should be disabled. Always strive to use the latest stable RabbitMQ version.

Volvo – stable and reliable: A system that must be highly available and cannot afford to lose messages should have durable queues and send persistent messages. Queues should still be kept short.

It is recommended that clustering is set up through quorum queues. If mirrored queues are already in use, add the lazy queue policy to get a more stable setup. Make sure that three or five nodes are used in the system to achieve high availability. When setting up a RabbitMQ cluster, split queues among different cores and into different nodes, using the Consistent Hash Exchange or sharding plugins to keep everything running smoothly and efficiently. Always strive to use the latest stable RabbitMQ version.

Now that the best practice tips have been covered, it's time to consider what should occur if and when something goes wrong. Monitoring the cluster and setting alarm policies are two very important finishing touches to any production environment.

Monitoring – querying the REST API

There are two main ways to retrieve live information when monitoring a RabbitMQ broker: one through the `rabbitmqctl` command-line tool and another through the **REST API** exposed over HTTP by the management console.

Any monitoring system can use these tools to collect metrics and report them to the log, analytics, reporting, and alert frameworks. Information could be pushed to external logging services for further analysis, as an example.

Since CC installed the management console, as described in Chapter 1, *A Rabbit Springs to Life*, the team opts to use the rich, well-documented API over the command line. RabbitMQ provides documentation at the `http://localhost:15672/` API on any node that has the management plugin installed. It is possible to retrieve the same raw metrics over the command line, albeit without graphics.

 Keep in mind that the management console is backed by the API, so anything that is seen and done within a browser can be done through the API.

RabbitMQ exposes a variety of different metric types for collection, as discussed in the preceding sections. These include, but are not limited to, the following:

- **Node status**: Testing the performance of RabbitMQ involves executing a set of commands to declare an aliveness-test queue and then publishing as well as consuming it. Set an alarm to fire if the command returns 0 (no messages consumed) through the appropriate request:

  ```
  curl -s
  http://cc-admin:******@localhost:15672/api/aliveness-test/cc-prod-v
  host | grep -c "ok"
  ```

- **Cluster size**: Testing the cluster size is useful for discovering network partitions. Set an alarm to fire if the cluster size is lower than expected:

  ```
  curl -s http://cc-admin:******@localhost:15672/api/nodes | grep -o
  "contexts" | wc -l
  ```

CC uses a `bash` script and Python to send an error when the number of nodes is less than expected.

- **Federation status**: Federated queues may become unlinked due to a restart or another issue. Check the active upstream links on the central log aggregation broker and raise an alarm if it's less than the optimal size (3, in CC's case), as follows:

```
curl -s
http://cc-admin:******@localhost:15672/api/federation-links/cc-prod
-vhost | grep -o "running" | wc -l
```

- **Queues' high watermarks**: Cloud-based brokers sometimes offer scale at low cost but with message limits. In other cases, message latency is an issue. Ensure that the number of available messages in a queue is below a certain threshold:

```
curl -s -f
http://cc-admin:******@localhost:15672/api/queues/cc-prod-vhost/tax
i-dlq | jq '.messages_ready'
```

In CC's case, they want to verify that the `taxi-dlq` queue has less than 25 messages. Otherwise, they raise an alarm indicating a bottleneck. Scripts need to handle a graceful failure if the queue does not exist.

- **Overall message throughput**: Monitoring the intensity of messaging traffic on a particular broker makes it possible to increase or decrease resources as required. Collect message rates with the following command:

```
curl -s
http://cc-admin:******@localhost:15672/api/vhosts/cc-prod-vhost |
jq '.messages_details.rate'
```

CC adds an alarm if the throughput threshold exceeds the upper limit of what one its brokers can withstand.

Some metrics come with rigid upper limits whose values are also available through the API. A recommendation is to raise an alarm whenever a threshold of 80 percent of the upper limit is reached. The following scripts return false when the alarm must be raised. These metrics include the following:

- **File descriptors**: Many OSes have file descriptor limits. The performance of the message persistence on the disk can be affected if not enough descriptors are available. The number of file descriptors used can be compared with the amount of available file descriptors:

```
curl -s
http://cc-admin:******@localhost:15672/api/nodes/rabbit@${host} |
jq '.fd_used<.fd_total*.8'
```

It is possible to increase the number of available file descriptors on macOS X and Linux. File descriptors are used to access other files. It's a good idea to check throughputs if this limit is exceeded as well.

- **Socket descriptors**: Socket descriptors maintain a handle to an individual socket for a connection. RabbitMQ stops accepting new connections if these descriptors are exhausted, which is a common issue with large clusters:

```
curl -s
http://cc-admin:******@localhost:15672/api/nodes/rabbit@${host} |
jq '.sockets_used<.sockets_total*.8'
```

Linux uses file descriptors for sockets, adjusting the count with the `ulimit` command. Using more channels and fewer connections, in line with best practices, helps to handle this issue as well.

- **Erlang processes**: There is an upper limit to the number of processes an Erlang virtual machine creates. Although typically near 1 million processes, each requires resources to run. The number of Erlang processes used can be compared with the Erlang process limit:

```
curl -s
http://cc-admin:******@localhost:15672/api/nodes/rabbit@${host} |
jq '.proc_used<.proc_total*.8
```

An OS thread is not created for each process. Still, each uses a lightweight stack and requires time to schedule and maintain.

- **Memory and disk space**: If memory or disk space is exhausted, RabbitMQ will not work properly – for example, flow control can be triggered. Check that there are sufficient resources and tune the hardware appropriately.
  The total amount of memory used should be less then 80 percent of the memory usage high watermark:

```
curl -s
http://cc-admin:******@localhost:15672/api/nodes/rabbit@${host} |
jq '.mem_used<.mem_limit*.8'curl -s
```

The disk free space limit should be compared to the current free disk space:

```
http://cc-admin:******@localhost:15672/api/nodes/rabbit@${host} |
jq '.disk_free_limit<.disk_free*.8'
```

In addition to metrics, a working instance runs the following programs:

- `rabbitmq-server`: This is obvious but should not be forgotten!
- `epmd`: The Erlang port mapper daemon, `epmd`, plays a critical role in clustering and networking. It is advisable to set up scripts to check that these services are running. List programs using `ps` on Linux or macOS X and `Get-Process` in Windows.

`ERROR REPORT` entries in the main log file reveal issues within the system. In Linux, RabbitMQ stores log files at `/var/log/rabbitmq/rabbit@<hostname>.log`. For more information, check the configuration file at `https://www.rabbitmq.com/logging.html#log-file-location`.

Summary

This chapter concludes the study of microservices built on RabbitMQ with an examination of best practices as well as monitoring. The book went through the application funnel for CC, beginning with the basic service and scaling. New features and processes were added with ease and without interruption to the CC application. Over time, CC's development team created a holistic, useful, reliable, long-life application. To avoid failures that could lead to bad user experience or even data loss, the CC team implemented a monitoring strategy. Collecting, logging, analyzing, and reporting metrics were outlined as CC formed an alert plan. Finally, the alert parameters were set up through the RabbitMQ management console.

Congratulations on completing your journey through this book! Armed with sufficient RabbitMQ wrangling skills, the next step is to create an instance for yourself. An easy way to get started with RabbitMQ is through the manager of the largest fleet of RabbitMQ clusters in the world – hosted RabbitMQ provider CloudAMQP.

Other Book You May Enjoy

If you enjoyed this book, you may be interested in these other book by Packt:

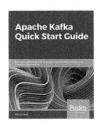

Apache Kafka Quick Start Guide
Raúl Estrada

ISBN: 978-1-78899-782-9

Learn how to clean your data and ready it for analysis

- How to validate data with Kafka
- Add information to existing data flows
- Generate new information through message composition
- Perform data validation and versioning with the Schema Registry
- How to perform message Serialization and Deserialization
- How to perform message Serialization and Deserialization
- Process data streams with Kafka Streams
- Understand the duality between tables and streams with KSQL

Leave a review - let other readers know what you think

Please share your thoughts on this book with others by leaving a review on the site that you bought it from. If you purchased the book from Amazon, please leave us an honest review on this book's Amazon page. This is vital so that other potential readers can see and use your unbiased opinion to make purchasing decisions, we can understand what our customers think about our products, and our authors can see your feedback on the title that they have worked with Packt to create. It will only take a few minutes of your time, but is valuable to other potential customers, our authors, and Packt. Thank you!

Index

Lightning Source UK Ltd.
Milton Keynes UK
UKHW021959260622
405003UK00005B/60